The
River Test

The River Test

Portrait of an English Chalkstream

by

Charles Bingham

H. F. & G. WITHERBY LTD

First published in Great Britain 1990 by
H. F. & G. WITHERBY LTD
14 Henrietta Street, London WC2E 8QJ

British Library Cataloguing in Publication Data
Bingham, Charles
    The River Test: portrait of an English
    chalkstream.
    1. Great Britain. Trout. Freshwater
    Angling
    I. Title
    799.1755

    ISBN 0-85493-189-9

Designed by Jonathan Newdick

Filmset in Garamond 156 and printed in Great Britain
by BAS Printers Limited, Over Wallop, Hampshire

Acknowledgements

I AM INDEBTED to all who helped in the preparation of this book. My progress up and down the river would not have prospered without the help of Brian Parker of the Bossington Estate and his father-in-law. Bill and Jean Waldron provided me with a second home close to the river. For advice, information and hospitality I am grateful to Ron Butcher, Mick Lunn, James Hancock, Bill Heller, Bernard Aldrich, Lorna Poole and Rupert Dawnay of Longparish.

My thanks are due to Maurice Jones, Rosemary Dunhill, the Hampshire County Archivist, and Sarah Lewin who discovered the 1823 Compton Notebook (2M37/560) which we include by permission of the Guardian of the Edwards Papers. The archivists also produced the Francis Frith photograph of Middlebridge, Romsey (56M71), the 1826 plan of the Houghton Club waters (10M55/73) and a lease of fishings in 1888 by Lord Mount Temple (105M70E3).

For permission to photograph on her estates, I am grateful to Marjorie, Countess of Brecknock. The Orvis Co., Prudential Property Services, Christie's and Christie's Scotland Ltd, *Shooting Times* and *Hampshire* provided photographs. I thank the archive collection of The John Lewis Partnership for permission to reproduce the Longstock fire insurance policy. Photographs, books and papers were loaned by Arthur and Anne Humbert, Robin Crawshaw, Fred Kemp, E. A. Lugg, Barry Diaper, Alf Harper, Jeff Smith, Antony Witherby, Justin Knowles, Terry Snelgrove, Brian Parker, Mary Snow, Michael Lickman, Tony Allen, Ralph Collins, Vic Foot and Ronald Coleby. I am grateful to them all. Special thanks to Tony Allen and Jonathan Newdick for their photographs.

Dedicated to the water-keepers of the Test and to Tony Allen, who introduced me to the river.

Contents

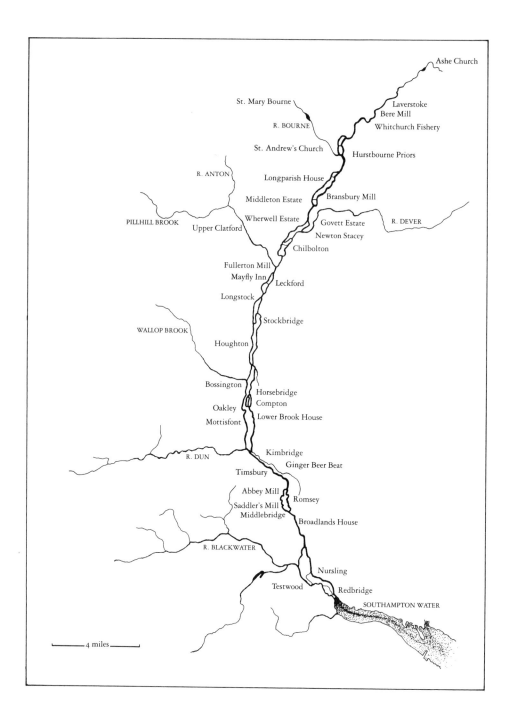

Introduction

THE RIVER TEST has been fished for centuries. Her alkaline waters have yielded quantities of trout, sea trout, salmon and other fish beyond the capacity of lesser streams. Tranquillity rises from the 'ever rolling stream' into the minds of anglers and those who pause beside this, the premier trout river of the world. The regal status of the Test is accepted, still, but all is not well. Here in past years, great and important men have sometimes solved problems besetting nations while sitting alone above the water buttercups. We visualize the Foreign Secretary, Viscount Grey of Fallodon, at the entrance to a thatched fishing hut, or John Waller Hills, who pondered on the nation's economy while knotting a Caperer to his cast. Some of these departed anglers have taken their place among the giants of fly-fishing history: Durnford, Francis Francis, Marryat, Halford and Skues have left their mark. England would be a poorer land without an Iron Blue braving the wind, a Houghton Ruby or a Lunn's Particular. The spinners still fall in the evening shadows as the sun sinks below the chalk downs.

Walking beside the river today in the steps of these masters we come to a fork, formed by twin streams flowing down towards us. Between the spreading arms of the river there stands a tree to which are nailed two arrowed signs. To the left we are directed to 'Rainbow Trout Fishery, guaranteed limit bag; contractors' lorries for boreholes, gravel pit and treatment works.' There is no ranunculus in the cloudy diminished stream, the bed of which is brown. The arrow pointing to the right reads 'Water Meadow, Wild Brown Trout Fishery, limit one brace.' In this stream there is a reasonable flow of clear water, swallows skim, and trout rise to hatching flies close to a wild-flowered path.

Today we stand at that junction. The problems are presented, the solutions also, on the signs. We know the stream we wish to fish, but soon the sign to the right may no longer offer the qualities we desire. 'I am grievously worried about the state of the river.' So says Bernard Aldrich of Broadlands after 35 years on the estate. In this book are recorded interviews with all the major river-keepers of the Test, from the source at Ashe to Redbridge on Southampton Water. Not one failed to *volunteer* increasing problems arising from nitrogen pollution and the resulting prolific growth of blanket weed. Crop growers, fish farmers, anglers, watercress producers, factory managements and landowners can contribute to the restoration of the river by some small sacrifice. Who will give a lead? Let anglers tread the right-hand path by expecting less. A brace of one pound wild brown trout a day would mean less pollution from the hatcheries. Two whole-finned, fine-tailed trout, wild and free. Think on this. It would be a start.

Enough of sad tidings. Let us view the river in past centuries and as it is today, noting that the old water wheel of the Bossington stews no longer irrigates the ponds – the level rarely reaches the blades due to abstraction in the valley. Nor is that all. I searched in vain for any flow in the bed of the Wallop Brook this summer, even where it joins the Test. It trickled again, a few days ago, in the first week of December. Many streams have been robbed by boreholes sucking from the aquifer. The Ordnance Survey $1\frac{1}{4}$ inch to 1 mile map of 'Winchester and Basingstoke area' is a cartographer's whimsical speculation in respect of the Bourne which is, today, shorter than shown by four miles. The village of St Mary Bourne knows little now of the lovely stream of Harry Plunket Greene, even as a winter bourne.

I approached the writing of this book aware that many have greater knowledge of some aspects of the river Test than myself. But it became clear that the task of compiling a volume on the fishing of the river over the years was not one for an authority on flies, or river maintenance, or an historian. The materials are too many and too diverse. The broad view is not for the specialist. Yet, small events make up the whole. Which fisherman may say, hand on heart, that he has not yielded to temptation as Col. Peter Hawker, with characteristic innovation, fell momentarily from grace on 24 January 1807: 'While beating the ditches for snipes I spied a very fine trout, which, with a piece of whipcord and a stick, I instantly snared; and he proved, when dressed, to be very well in season.' With such material to hand from the past, and the generous help of many living on the river today, I made a start.

In the 19th century men had time: to write, record and experiment. Which of the many fishing masters of that era should be mentioned? If I write of my survey at Broadlands, Leckford and Laverstoke, but leave out Marsh Court and the little reaches, this is because pages cannot be found for every yard. Who would hope to equal the fine prose of great angling writers of the past? Diffidence troubled me. The thought then formed in my mind that these problems would plague any country author set to such a task. I took comfort from Hawker who robustly defended his diary:

> 'If, therefore, this elegant piece of syntax should fall into the hands of a word-catcher, I can only say that I will correct literary errors as fast as he may find them, conditionally that he gives me a bottle of wine for each; and if he meets with any such mistake subsequent to my revision, I will, as a punishment for my ignorance, give him a dozen of wine, and if a dandy a new pair of stays. By saying this, far be it from me to presume where I have not the slightest pretensions, but merely act on the defensive against some of those half-educated machines who are so fond of saying "This fellow cannot write English", and who seek for the leaves on a tree rather than the effect of the landscape; in short, people who look at their words as a lady would examine a piece of Brussels lace.'

Colonel Hawker's writing has endured: his fowling piece smokes in his left hand as he writes with his right, or so one might imagine; his study the workshop of both author and angler. In turn, and at times in comparison with those angling writers of the past, I have attempted to review fishing activities on the Test, past and present.

On 24 February 1989 I visited Maurice Jones who was Managing Director of Leckford Estates from 1948 until his retirement in 1980. After lunch he remarked: 'Your problem, Charles, will be what to leave out of this book.' Months later, with old books, fishing leases, maps and stories gathered, I remembered his observation as we looked across the river from The Grange, Longstock, headquarters of old Longstock Fishing Club. He was right. I ask your tolerance of any lack of judgement in my selection.

CHARLES BINGHAM *Dartmoor   April 1990*

The Source of the Test

6 JULY 1989

HIS NAME IS ALBERT HOLMES, but everyone calls him Bert. We met as he walked his dog, Bess, close to the church at Ashe. He is the oldest inhabitant, having worked as a tractor driver at Lower Ashe Farm since 1940. For 50 years he has been within sight of the source of the Test. 'Is there a spring bubbling out of the ground?'

He looked at me rather sadly.

'People come here all through the year to look. In winter they used to see a muddy pond. In July just mud. It flowed a bit in early spring, starting in February, and then it just dried up as the months went by. They've dug it out now to make a lake. Trout live there.'

There was nothing more to see or say. I looked across the field; earth movers were there, scraping out the pond.

Laverstoke

DAVE WALFORD — TROUT-KEEPER
22 SEPTEMBER 1989

IF YOU WALK DOWNSTREAM from the source of the Test at Ashe the first head-keeper you would meet would be Dave Walford. If you were a 'ne'er-do-well' you would be wise to remove yourself from the path by the river; Dave is large and formidable. He lives at Bere Mill, between Whitchurch and Overton, which I reached by driving across the river 100 yards upstream on the Christmas Cake bridge – not a bad description for this ornate stone structure.

The mill was built in 1710 and for the first two years ground corn. In 1712 a Huguenot refugee, Henry de Portal, arrived at Bere Mill and started making paper instead of milling cereals. After three years he moved to Laverstoke Mill where he continued this trade in conjunction with the Bere operation. After a while all production was concentrated at Laverstoke. A new mill was built at Overton in 1949 and this operates today making paper for Bank of England notes. The bank-note side of the business is operated by Portals Holdings, while the estate management is under the control of Portals Property, Dave's employers. Sir Francis Portal died in 1987.

The river starts at Ashe, where the original source is now within a recently constructed lake which, as we spoke, was empty of water due to the summer drought. The stream then runs through Polhampton farm which has recently been sold by Portals Property together with Dave's top beat which he still manages. His responsibility for the river continues for $4\frac{1}{2}$ miles downstream through Overton, Laverstoke and Freefolk to 300 yards below Bere Mill where he meets the Whitchurch Fishery of Fred Kemp. The river is shallow and all fishable from one bank. There are no carriers, just two small side streams joining the main river. The position carries a heavy responsibility; whatever he does affects all those down-

OPPOSITE *Dave Walford. Eel grid at Bere Mill.*

13

stream: 'You've only got to let a bit of weed go, or colour the water, and the phone's ringing.'

Before he came to Bere Mill 18 years ago he had had a varied career, with fishing his recreation. When he was a youngster his father owned some water meadows adjacent to Andover. These were excavated in 1943 for gravel; subsequently the pits became the Charlton Fishery. One of his father's friends was Frank Sawyer, the famous keeper from the upper Avon. Just after the war Frank netted his river and transferred many hundreds of fish, grayling, roach and others, to the Charlton water. Dave watched Frank, talked with him and gathered much water wisdom. But life was not all fishing. After leaving school he started work as a police cadet and followed it with National Service in the Royal Air Force. Returning to the police he became restless, worked in his father's transport business, but fishing and fisheries plucked at his heart. At times the Test called and he would help at Capt. Andrew Wills' estate at Longparish. One day the Captain telephoned 'Would Dave become the Middleton Estate head river keeper?' For four years Capt. Wills was his employer before the Bere Mill position became vacant.

We walked to his hatchery inside and below the mill where there is a brick pen through which the river flows. I peered into the depths of the pen where large ghostly shadows, his brood fish, patrolled, circulating in a dignified manner until he threw in some pellets. The rainbows rose to slash at the food, ripping through the water. Not so the browns of 2, 4, 6 or even 8 lbs. They rolled up, sipped and sank away at a leisurely pace. At the end of October and in November they will be stripped for the hatchery in the mill which provides baby fish for his trout farm and the river. The brown trout ova hatch after 34 days, rainbows after 29; they absorb the yolk sac in about two or three weeks, and are then in the 'swim-up' stage of one month's feeding which precedes 'planting out'. Transfer to the river is done when the fry are $\frac{3}{4}$ inch long. Dave does this with a watering can: 'I go along the river squirting small fry out of the spout.' He does not buy in trout, neither does he stock the river with grown fish. His is a natural system which results in a catch averaging $1\frac{1}{4}$ lb with an occasional two-pounder, and they are all as wild as the wind is free.

His rods are mainly guests of the company and a few tenants who have been on the river for years. At the same time days are available for anyone who rings up, 'It is true to say that the river is open to all.' His is a fine stretch of water, moderately fished, 'There is one thing which spoils good fishing – over fishing.'

I asked about salmon. 'They do not come up here. When I was at Long-parish I used to see them spawning at Lower Mill, by the bridge. I still look over but never see them today.' Was this due to a reduction in water purity, I asked. He takes a long view of the river's quality and the fish therein. 'In the 1890s the river was well populated with coarse fish: pike, dace, grayling. In many places it was an open sewer. Those living by the river poured it straight in. This does not happen today.' He has talked to some of the pollution officers and is of the opinion, from the sewage angle, that the river is cleaner than it was 100 years ago. Additional nitrogen is in a different category, probably accounting for the present heavy growths of blanket weed and, he suspects, a reduction in the runs of eels. 'Fish farms are a problem and have been for some time, but the fish farmers are responsible people and are trying to get their act together.' He feels that keeping the river clean depends substantially on a good winter weed cut clearing the bed; water can then scour out the mud. If weed is allowed to rot silt builds up and good young weed does not grow. His water is clear almost throughout the year except for some discoloration below the paper mill. The flow below the mill is monitored by Southern Water and Portals' own team of chemists, 'Even so, when you have a factory at the head of a river, you will have the occasional accident.'

On water flow he has noticed a reduction. 'There has been a population explosion in Basingstoke and the surrounding area. All these people need water from boreholes. Millions and millions of gallons daily.' Before they built the fish farm Dave arranged a visit by a water diviner who had only made one mistake in 400 'finds'. 'He became very excited and said that at one spot there was an underground ocean. He used an apple-wood fork, not hazel. We all had a go and it always worked.' There is now a borehole for the hatchery at the mill. The water is pumped out of the hole, goes through the system, and is then piped into the river.

Close to the mill is an eel grid which he had set the previous night. Five large specimens lay stranded on the iron bars. Only a few are sold, most of the catch being smoked for the company. Eels start to run on 'the first dark' (when there is no moon) in June. By August his run is over. There are fewer than there used to be. He knows this not only from the reduced catch but because he no longer sees them feeding on warm nights or, at least, not so frequently. This year he missed the first run due to a local thunderstorm upstream. 'They always run when the river fills after a storm.' There was no rain at Bere Mill but higher up his underkeeper had to open the hatches to prevent flooding; a high proportion of his eels went down on the flood without the trap being set. By the time Dave discovered the situation it was too late. 'Bere Mill remained dry as a bone.'

On flies: 'The higher you go on the river the smaller things become. As the Americans say "You match the hatch". I use very small dressings of a Lunn's Particular, just one and a half turns of hackle on a No. 16 or No. 18 hook. When the duns are on I pop the wings up and when the spent's on I pop them down.' He actually squeezes the wings into position with his fingers. At times he changes to a Kite's Imperial. On this section of the river there are no mayfly. Blue-winged olives are present, all the pale wateries and a very small dark fly with slate blue wings which is not an iron blue. 'There has not been a hatch of iron blue for many years.' No grannom. Hawthorn? 'Yes.' Anything else? 'Occasionally we get a good fall of flying ants – I then dart indoors out of the way.'

Nymph fishing is allowed after mid-June. 'I think nymph fishing is marvellous. I've had several dry fly purists come here and I've taught them to fish the nymph. That's all they do now, not because it's easier but because they are fascinated.'

We then talked about wildlife. In 1956 he was sitting by the Charlton lake. Hearing a whistling noise he looked up to see six otters, adults and young, swimming in the gravel pits at the top of the river Anton. He had noticed dead fish and half-eaten eels on an island but until the otters were revealed did not know the predator. They were then disturbed by people who came to look; he only saw them once more. A dead one was found by the side of the road at Wherwell a few years ago. This otter may have escaped from those used in filming *Tarka the Otter,* some of which was shot in a fenced-off area in Laverstoke Park. 'My wife went to the Hebrides to try to catch otters for the film, but without success, so some from Philip Ware's Otter Trust were used. I believe one escaped.' If Dave found one causing trouble today in his fish farm he would just trap it and move it elsewhere, 'People are much more concerned today with looking after wildlife. At one time they shot kingfishers – now we have many pairs. I can look out of my kitchen window and there is always one sitting on a little bridge. I have found their nests in a chalk bank in a little stream.'

Before leaving we walked below the mill to his weed pen. This is a metal barred grid, 100 yards long, which crosses the river at an angle. Above the grid is the pen. Not only does this trap weed, 'Anyone could fish 200 yards below and be unaware of a weed cut', it also acts as the fishes' larder. Insects breed in the sluggish water, trout feed and mallard too are attracted by the insect life; four rose into the air as we watched, and a kingfisher piped a thin call in an adjoining ditch. The pen is heaven for a gourmand trout, 'Frogs swim here at their peril – some are sucked from sight.'

Trout ponds at Bere Mill.

Whitchurch Fishery

FRED KEMP — TROUT-KEEPER
30 AUGUST 1989

THE WHITCHURCH FISHERY of 'Chips' Keswick runs from Winchester Road to just below Bere Mill where the Laverstoke Estate takes over. Fred has been in charge of the $1\frac{3}{4}$ miles of double bank water for 17 years. His house, The Fishing Cottage, is tucked back behind trees and shrubs in Test Road. I drove past, missing the sign, and had to double back. He and his wife welcomed me with coffee, opened the sliding glass door of the drawing room from which we stepped out onto a lawn which spread to the river. It would be difficult to find a more convenient riverside place to live: step out of the front door to walk into town; open the sliding door and Fred, in ten seconds, is at his place of work.

In the house he picked up a framed photograph of himself with two boys on the grass, a picture which had been taken by the river. 'Know who those are?.' I had to admit that I was at a loss, and yet! 'That's Prince William and Prince Harry. I took them fishing. They're sturdy tough little lads.' We sat and talked. Fred was born in the New Forest. He always liked fly fishing and the exciting days he spent after grayling at Bossington with Tim Baker, the keeper. He thought Tim had an idyllic life, 'But I've since found out it is not quite so idyllic as I thought.' Tim told him there was a river-keeper's job on offer at Whitchurch. At his interview he was asked if he knew anything about keepering, and had to reply 'Very little, but I know about country pursuits.' He was then asked if he drank, to which he replied 'Yes.' 'That was about the total of the interview for I was told at once that I could have the job because "I was the first who did not know more than Izaak Walton" and the only applicant who was not teetotal.'

We progressed to talking about the river, fly life and fishing. Although his water is double bank, they only fish one side. The other side, left wild, gives good cover for fly life: 'You don't want both banks looking like a bowling green.' They do not wade much – sometimes when grayling fishing, for which he uses a Pheasant Tail Nymph and a Sawyer Bug. A most success-ful nymph has a thin dressing of red fluorescent wool. In four hours once Fred and a friend caught 86 grayling. They used the Pheasant Tail nymph, Sawyer's Bug and a Corixa.

For trout he recommends an Iron Blue, but if he had to pick one fly it would be a No. 18 Grey Duster. This has a body of light rabbit's fur and a hint of blue under-fur. The hackle is stiff badger cock with a dark centre. Some of the best flies he has come across are American: very small, sizes 18 and 20. They are expensive, but of excellent quality, and should be used with fine nylon. 'In Scotland, for salmon, a friend of mine says "big fly, big fish", but here, for trout, I've found the opposite is the case on the Test.' This is confirmed by large rainbow trout; he puts a few into a lake up the river. 'When you put them in you can catch them on anything. Within a month they are more difficult than a wild brown. You must go down to a small fly. When they sip tiny things off the surface I use a little Adams, grey wool body, spent wings of two grizzle feathers and a hackle of red grizzle cock of which a few fibres can be used for the tail. With the spent wings you could term it semi-dry. It gets a bit damp – if you know what I mean!.'

Fred studies fly life and the rise forms of trout. His understanding of fish vision was widened by reading Vincent C. Marinaro, born in 1911 in Reynoldsville, Pennsylvania. His book, *In the Ring of the Rise,* is a real life venture into the world of the trout. The pages on fish vision, flies, real and artificial, tackle and rivers are accompanied by superb photographs of fish in action. Fred loaned me his copy, inscribed by a grateful American visitor: 'For Fred Kemp. With gratitude for his own fine observation and river keeping.'

Fred's boss does not let rods, and the water is thus lightly fished, but he stocks a few browns and rainbows, none of them over-large. Fingerling brown trout are also introduced every three years, and the wild stock remains good. The greatest threat to his part of the river is house building, 'Not just one house, but hundreds. They just O.K. building anywhere and the water abstraction increases.' Fred has been able to counteract less water and reduced flows by narrowing his river. 'If you halve the width you double the flow. That's the only way around the problem. They couldn't do it lower down the river, but here the watercourse is smaller and not so deep.'

Treated sewage is also a problem. Even so, on his beat, high up the valley, the river runs clear. 'Keepers moan about dirty, cloudy water lower down the Test, and this is true, but here, at the Whitchurch Fishery, it is always clear. Even in mid-winter it runs like gin, unless someone is working higher up the valley.' Pollution from the roads worries him, 'Everything runs straight into the river. If we had an oil tanker turn over . . . .'

There is a problem with blanket weed which was not apparent when he came to the river. Intensive farming close to the river bank is the suspected reason. Nitrogenous fertilizer applications and leaching into the river are a little better than they were four years ago. 'They even spread it from aeroplanes. I've been working in the river and had pellets fall around me.'

He cuts all his weed with a Turk scythe, but would like to develop a floating machine weed cutter which could be operated by hand and pushed up the river.

Electric fishing for coarse fish is done with a boat which he pushes up the river in chest waders. Before 1976 there were no pike then, that year, he had about 20, all in one place close to a bridge. Someone might have tipped them in for one reason or another, but Fred had them all out within two years. From 1979 to the present only one pike has been turned up by the electric fishing boat. There are no dace and salmon do not come above Longparish to spawn.

Leaving the house we walked to the river. Downstream is Fulling Mill. Years ago this was the property of James Robertson Justice whose young son was tragically drowned in the river. There are also short stretches owned by Lord Denning, retired Master of the Rolls, and John Clarke, the Hampshire coroner. Upstream, within 100 yards, is the waterside Fishing Lodge of his employer. Several hundred yards beyond this is Town Mill, home of Ronald Eastman who directed and photographed the RSPB video *Kingfisher*. Scenes were also shot there of *Tarka The Otter* in which the stars were three Malayan otters and Bill Travers.

Fred held that the banks of his river are too low for nesting kingfishers. If he wanted a pair to nest he would build a wall of turf, 3 or 4 feet high, between an expanded metal frame with 4-inch mesh. The birds would soon tunnel into this to lay their clutch of small white eggs.

Longparish

COLONEL PETER HAWKER OF LONGPARISH HOUSE

LONGPARISH HOUSE resembles a small French château. Here lived Colonel Peter Hawker, veteran of the Peninsular War (when he was seriously wounded) and one of our greatest wildfowlers and trout fishermen. It was here that, in 1853, he made the last of 51 years of diary entries. From these entries the angler of today may visualize a kindred spirit. In 1953 I fished the Test five miles downstream at Leckford when Ernie Mott was keeper. The same year a wigeon fell to my gun at Keyhaven where Hawker had his fowling cottage. He used a gunning punt; I a canoe and 3 inch Magnum 12 bore. He cast his flies downstream – today we cast up-river.

So, what changes have taken place with the passing of the years? The first is that the Colonel caught far more trout than any of us would wish, or be able, to achieve today. In the Diary summary is the statement 'The trout killed in the fifty years of the Colonel's sporting life could not have been less than twelve thousand.' When I read his entry of 27 May 1807, 'Longparish. Killed 20 brace of trout with a fly in three hours.' I was sceptical for that is a trout every four-and-a-half minutes. But, reading on, I came to accept the Diary's reliability. Entries such as:

'1814 April 12. Went out fly fishing, and, notwithstanding a bright sun the whole time, I in a few hours killed 36 trout. N.B. – My flies were (what I always use) the yellow dun at bottom, and red palmer bob.'
'1814. April 15. 28 trout.'
'1814, April 16. 24 trout (average weight above 1 lb each, and many of them weighed 1½ lb). Also a great many fair sized ones which I threw in. I had all this admirable sport in less than two hours and a half, and the weight of these fish was so much that they were quite a burthen to carry home. In the evening I was ludicrously amused with throwing a fly on horseback, which answers as well as on foot; though I then

caught no fish large enough to save, owing to the wind having shifted to a cold quarter.'

He continued to fish intermittently over the next fortnight, taking a total of 100 brace in 11 days, and, on '28 April, 13 trout average weight 1¼ lb each fish.'

He adds: 'N.B. I, of course, have reckoned only those fish which I killed; namely, such as were ¾ lb and upwards. But had I killed all the small ones and added them to my number, it would have amounted to between 400 and 500 fish.'

Such catches could not be made today, and, if achievable, could scarcely be approved. The circumstances were different then: the river virtually unfished and thus the trout uneducated. No 'nine to five' for Hawker. He lived the life of a sporting country squire. Yet he was not greedy, for there is no doubt the catch would have been eaten by his extensive household – or given away.

'1820. April 1. Killed 5 brace of trout. This is the first tolerable day I have had, though I have killed a few for dinner most days for some time; but now, as the river is my own, I never care about taking any but the best fish, which I kill only when I want them, and therefore do not take the trouble to keep any account of the great number that I catch.'

Given away they were, or eaten, but there is no doubt that the Colonel was competitive:

'1823. June 28. Longparish. For these several years past I have never cared about fishing further than to supply my friends, and then lay aside my rod whenever I made up my basket; but finding that it now becomes a kind of trumpery theme for reputation to kill so many fish, in order to chatter about the performance, I availed myself of about five hours fine weather this day and honestly bagged 46 killable trout, besides a great many thrown in; my first 35 were all particularly fine fish, the largest 1¾ lb, which is the very best size our river is now likely to produce.'

He writes little of his methods of fishing, being more concerned with keeping an accurate record of the bag. It appears that he cast his fly downstream, or two flies in rough weather, the bob to anchor the point, and had little to do with the blow line. This must be the case for he often writes of 'throwing the fly'. '13 July 1810. 2½ brace of trout (largest 1½ lb weight) besides many thrown in, not wanting. N.B. Caught fish by throwing the fly as I sat in the phaeton.' Fishing from the phaeton carriage was, no doubt, an intermittent necessity when his wound became inflamed. On 16 April 1814 he threw the fly while on horseback.

Clearly Hawker practised casting, or 'whipping' as it was then called, and not 'blowing'. It is odd that he does not refer to blowing which was being practised in those years by the Rev. Richard Durnford a few miles away at Chilbolton. Perhaps he did not care to rely on the wind; this would be in character for so independent a spirit. Perhaps he tried this method and gave it up, and this seems likely from the following entry:

'1816 July 31st. Went over to Ponton's at Stockbridge. Found the fly fishing, as it almost always is at this celebrated though infamously bad place, not worth a penny. The cockney-like amusement of bobbing with a live mayfly is all that this miserable river does for; indeed, scarcely a fish ever moves till about the last quarter of an hour that you can see to throw a line.'

As is the case today he had to endure a period of unproductive fishing when the mayfly ceased or there were too many on the water:

'1816 June 15. 10 trout. Fishing very indifferent, owing to the trout being glutted with the mayfly and small gnats.' And, '1817 June 11. Went over to Ponton's, where after two days fishing I caught but 4 brace of trout; and so execrable is the Stockbridge fishing that this was literally called good sport. The fish are immensely large, but so flabby and soft as to be scarcely worth eating. We worked the real mayfly as well as the artificial.'

Do we not today recall the excitement of being offered a rod on a stretch of the Test? Some of us have been able to rent or purchase a few hundred yards of the river, enjoying the feeling that we have, for a time, a little of England's premier trout river to call our own. The Colonel's Diary records his own satisfaction:

'1818 February 23. Having purchased the celebrated fishery of Mr Widmore, I this day bought Mr Sutton's lease, with which it was encumbered, and became possessed in fee simple of one of the first trout rivers in the world. Shot 1 hare and 3 jack snipes; afterwards went fly fishing on my newly purchased river, and when the snow was a foot deep, I caught a dish of fish for dinner in about half an hour, which proved in capital season. At night it thawed, and we had another attack from torrents of rain.'

In Hawker's day there was no close season for brown trout. He frequently refers to fish being 'in good season' by which he must mean not gravid or in spawning colours. Later the same year he again took advantage of his newly acquired water:

'1818 July 10. In about an hour I killed with a fly before the house three large baskets of trout, which averaged $1\frac{1}{4}$ lb each fish.
N.B. As the whole fishery which goes through our premises was purchased by me of Mr Widmore previous to this season, I never made a regular day's fishing, but merely went angling for a few hours before dinner and seldom failed to kill a large dish of trout whenever we wanted them. I therefore have this year kept no account, though, were I to include nets and all, I should perhaps have to note down about a ton weight of trout, etc.; this is about the half of what the previous occupier took in a season by dragging.'

What is probably our best description of this outstanding angler and lover of the Test comes from Sir Ralph Payne-Gallwey in 1893:

'In figure Colonel Hawker was over six feet and strikingly handsome, and up to the end of his life was very erect. He was, no doubt, somewhat of an egotist, but it was in a good-natured way, and a confirmed but amusing grumbler against his personal ill-luck, and his constant enemy the weather; he was, however, an instructive and witty companion, and a conversationalist who always commanded attention, particularly when he related his long and varied experiences of sport, the adventures of his younger days in the Peninsular War, or conversed on music, literature, and travel.'

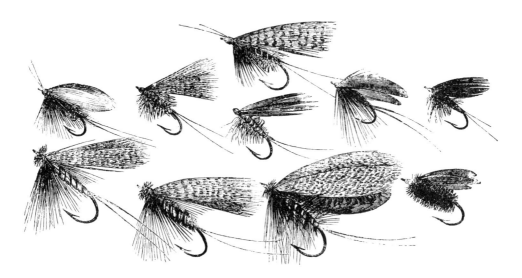

Longparish House. Alf Harper trimming verges.

Longparish

ALF HARPER — TROUT-KEEPER
8/9 AUGUST 1989

THE INTRODUCTION TO THIS BOOK confronts the angler, and those who live and work in the Test valley, with a choice: land a brace of free-spawned one pound brown trout a day, or six portly rainbows stocked at full weight from the over-populated stew. This modest catch could be the base line, a reasonable expectation, to be improved upon by river-keepers with an understanding of natural ways. To achieve this a keeper must be different and a non-conformist. Alf Harper of Longparish treads his own path.

What has Alf done to make his water appeal to me more than any other stretch of the river that I have visited in my investigations of the valley? The answer is that he has interfered with the river and his fish less than almost anyone else. The banks are not mown close; bushes overhang and caterpillars descend from them on silken threads; moorhens nest; rainbow trout are not welcome; he rears no brown trout but buys in fry.

Do not imagine that Alf is idle – he has few moments to spare and yet he does not hurry, proceeding down the river in a stately rolling gait. His is a natural pace for himself and the trout, and natural is the system by which he sustains his pheasant shoot. Yes, he sees to the shoot as well. No bought in birds for Alf. He catches-up his hens in January in the old manner in traps like unspillable inkwells, pens fifteen hens to a cock, takes forty eggs from each hen and then frees them to nest in the wild. From egg, to chick, to poult, to the woods, he oversees their progress.

The results of his methods should encourage us all. Brian Cook, one of his rods, reported his 1988 catch as follows:

In 37 fishing days my guests and I killed:
1. 167 brown trout, average weight just over 1 lb 5 oz
2. 10 rainbrow trout, largest 2 lb 4 oz, smallest 8 oz
3. 37 grayling, largest 1 lb 8 oz

This is an average of just over 2 brace a day. Of these only 14 were over 2 lb, and two exceeded 3 lb. There is no doubt Brian and his guests had magnificent, challenging fishing.

Alf Harper is 56 and came down from Durham in 1968. Like Bill Hawkins of Wherwell (page 48) he was a miner. His first taste of the South was at Barton Stacey, further down the river, while in the army. Following this he married and took over Rooksbury Mill Fishery on the river Anton at Andover. These lakes were excavated for gravel in 1970. He managed Rooksbury until 1975, and then came to Longparish House where he is in his fifteenth season as keeper. His employer was Colonel Dawnay who died on 30 January 1989.

As a boy he became a rabbit catcher at 15 and then started on gamekeeping. 'Where did you learn about fishing?.' He grinned, recalling happy clandestine memories. 'From the other side of the fence!'

The river divides at Longparish and Alf has over two miles of both parallel streams, a total of five miles of double bank water. He told me that the Test is only 29 miles long, 'But if you ask all the keepers how many miles they have, and add them all together, the river becomes as long as the Mississippi.'

This water is fished by six full season rods and an occasional day rod. They do not fish from the banks but by wading in thigh boots or chest waders. This is the first fishery on the upper Test where the banks are not cut and mown and the water is sufficiently shallow to wade. Much common land is close to the river, and if the banks are mown they become the haunt of picnic parties.

All the trout are wild browns. Some are introduced as fry or fingerlings, and rainbows are taken out as vermin when they come into the fishery from up and down the river. If the water has been very heavily fished he might put in 100 or 150 purchased stock fish, but they would only be 12 oz to 1 lb. Such a stocking on so extensive a water has no marked effect on his policy of providing truly wild fishing. I told Alf that his was the first natural fishery I had come across in my journey up the river. He replied that free spawning kept the water well stocked and 'If you have big stocked fish you have no small wild ones. Anything over 2 lb and they tend to be cannibal and eat all your little fish. The result is a shortage of natural browns in the future.'

I mentioned that Col. Hawker used to net the river in the 1800s and, in addition to trout, take large quantities of dace. These small fish, the schoolboy's trout, have had a fascination for me since catching them on a wet fly (and eating them in my study) while at school. In the last five years he has taken no more than half-a-dozen annually, while removing 3–4000 grayling. The coarse fish are taken by electric fishing and netting, but only two pike have been encountered in his 15 years: 'He doesn't have much chance in the fast water.'

There are a few crayfish, but the numbers seem to be declining. Three years ago the Ministry of Agriculture set crayfish traps, but only caught two or three. He believes American signal crayfish are creeping in and the result may be 'as the red squirrel was driven out by the grey'. A few salmon spawn after the trout have cut their redds at the end of October. In Col. Hawker's day there was regular mention of jack snipe – they are still about, also common snipe and the elusive water rail. That morning he had seen a kingfisher and 'more than enough herons'. No mink, no otters. He had thought of re-introducing otters because 'There are enough eels in the river to sustain them. If there are eels they'll not touch a trout.' He has badgers and from time to time catches 'the old boar' in a fox wire. There must be a special relationship between that badger and the keeper for he holds him down with a forked stick while cutting off the wire, and each expects to meet again.

Weed cutting is done with a hand scythe in the shallow water. All growth is cut out at the end of the season to allow the winter flows to scour the river bed. There are problems with weed – at times Alf doesn't have any! 'This year it grew prolifically until the end of February and then, all of a sudden, it just went. Longparish Common was denuded.' It occurred to me that this might be due to defoliants used by upstream watercress farmers. The weed returned in June.

We talked about the fly life and the fishing during his season from 1 May to 30 September. 'The fly life starts very dull and then improves. We have all the usuals: iron blue, gnats, and the blue-winged olive in June. Terrific hatches of mayfly these last five years, usually from the last week of May to the end of the first week in June. Sedges in the evening.' The artificials mentioned in Brian Cook's return are; Greenwell, Beacon Beige, Lunn's Particular, Pheasant Tail, Adams ('that's like a small brown upright'), Houghton Ruby, Kite's Imperial and a green nymph. There is also the surprise entry, 'Footballer'. To prevent raised eyebrows I give John Veniard's dressing of this pattern (which was invented by Geoffrey Bucknall):

HOOK   12–16

BODY   Alternate windings of black and white horsehair, wound well round bend of hook. A black and white barred effect is required.

THORAX   Mole fur

HEAD   Two turns of bronze peacock herl.

On 9 August we went from Alf's cottage to Longparish House and stood on a river bridge to the south. The house has been altered over the years. Rupert Dawnay, the present owner, showed me a copy of a painting executed in 1798 by Peter Hawker. Looking north from the bridge, and to the right of the house, is a small brown brick building, originally a private chapel, but later a rod room. In the river, downstream of the house, is Roper's Island, named after one of the Dawnays' dogs who there helped himself to pheasants. Also in this area is an old duck decoy and a place where Hawker kept a gunning punt. Rupert took me to the house to see one of Hawker's punt guns which had exploded. The accident is recorded in his diaries:

'19 February 1818. When firing at some geese my stanchion gun of about 96 lb weight was literally blown to atoms from the breaching to nearly the end of the stock, and though the lock and other appendages were dealing death and destruction in every quarter, and I was for a considerable time on fire while with a pound of gunpowder in my pocket, thank God not the slightest injury was sustained, further than the end of one of the oars being blown off. Nothing but the kind interference of Providence, and my invention for firing this gun, could possibly have saved my life.'

Following the Colonel's death in 1853 the house continued in the Hawker family, sometimes through the female line, until 1919 when it was purchased by Rupert Dawnay's grandfather, who, apparently, would not let anyone fish the river until they could cast a fly onto a handkerchief placed on the lawn.

Harrowing the riverbed at Longparish, 1905.

Middleton Estate

JEFFREY SMITH — TROUT-KEEPER
3 OCTOBER 1989

WE WALKED FROM JEFF'S HOUSE to Fishery Lodge. This romantic circular building reminds me of a broch, but there are differences. The Lodge is beside the Test, not placed on a crag in northern Scotland; it was built of wood in 1926 and not of stone in prehistoric times. There is not another construction like it on the river. 'Ours is the only hut with hot water and a flushing loo.' There is also a gun-room, a wash basin, stairs to a rugged rod- and dining-room, wooden tables and chairs, a fireplace, and a balcony over the river. 'Two of our rods stripped off one day and jumped into the river from the balcony for a £50 bet.... Yes, I light a fire on shooting days, then go beating, and return to see that all is burning well for lunch.' I commented on the central chandelier of stags' horn. 'Capt. Wills made that.'

On one wall is a rhyme, written out and framed by Jeff's wife, Barbara:

'Behold the fisherman. He riseth early in the morning and disturbeth the whole household. Mighty are the preparations, and he goeth forth full of hope. When the day is far spent he returneth smelling of strong drink, and the truth is not in him.'

We went out onto the balcony and looked down at the river which appeared from under a wooden barn, and flowed into a deep pool. A water-powered turbine in the barn is coupled to a circular saw. 'The estate timber was cut there. It is still in order, but not used today.' In the river we saw watercress running to seed, also starwort, ranunculus and mares' tails. Jeff doesn't eat the watercress because it may hold liver fluke. 'If you get that you're in Queer Street.' We noticed much blanket weed, both static and drifting down the river. 'See that, I've got strings of it, about forty or fifty yards long.'

32

We noticed a large grayling: 'Look at his orange dorsal fin and split tail. I wouldn't like to see all the grayling gone. I don't fish for trout, only grayling. I love that. I don't eat them – they're an oily greasy fish. But some people prefer a grayling to a trout. I let people fish for grayling in the winter.'

Many brown trout swam in the pool together with one or two rainbows which had arrived from elsewhere and 'two finnock – they've been here most of the summer.' Two rainbows were caught in his water in the 1989 season but they do not spawn in the river. Salmon spawn there in December, in reducing numbers, they work their way through the turbine and continue on upstream. We saw two trout cutting a redd.

In the rod-room we talked about Jeff's career. He moved up-river to Middleton from Wherwell where he worked for 15 years under Bill Hawkins (page 48). He is now in his third season as head-keeper. I questioned his origins and how he came to know about the river when he lived in Yorkshire, working as a miner. Had he visited the river? 'No, but I had a book as a boy. I still have it. It was given to me one Christmas. *Mr Crabtree Goes Fishing* by Bernard Venables. He lives near here. I was 10 years old at the time. The book was mainly about coarse fishing but touched on trout. There was a double page of artificial flies. One fly had the note "This fly was invented by the famous river-keeper Alfred Lunn." I thought "What's a river-keeper? I've never heard of them." So I started to read about the Test.'

For a number of years he answered advertisements, trying for a keeper's job. He applied for the Wherwell position at the same time as Bill Hawkins, but without a driving licence could not be accepted. Then Paul O'Toole, the Wherwell head-keeper, died and the estate sent for him. For 15 years he trained under Bill, having worked with him in the same Yorkshire coal mine. When the Middleton head-keeper Alfie Groves became ill the estate offered him the position. Richard Wills, son of the Captain, took him on and is his present employer.

We talked about his river. Four times a season he stocks with brown trout of between 1 lb and 2 lb. In May he purchases brown trout fry from Dave Walford at Laverstoke (page 13), from these a good stock of $\frac{3}{4}$ lb wild fish populate the beats. His water is about four miles in length. There are two streams: the 'main', which is at the fishing hut, and the 'half-water', a carrier which comes off the main river and rejoins it above the A303 trunk road. The army has the left bank of the 'half-water'. There are six beats on the 'main' syndicate water. The seventh beat, the Home Beat at the fishing hut, is kept for the Wills family and day ticket holders. There are two beats on the 'half-water'.

The 'half-water' is fished by season rods who have one named day a week. They fish the two beats on alternate weeks. Season rods on the 'main' water can fish seven days a week if they wish, on a beat rotating basis. Jeff advertises his day rods and has responses in the spring. He does not book day rods until February when the weed cutting dates are made known, those days are not let. In addition to trout there are a few shoals of dace and roach in the 'half-water'. Pike are removed by wiring and electric fishing. Grayling are controlled by winter fishing, which is let by the day.

During his 18 years on the river he has seen a reduction in both water flows and fly life. Water quality is declining. 'Too much nitrogen is put on the fields. I remember when they put a bag here and a bag there on the land. . . . Now tons go everywhere and get washed into the river. Take the water that is pumped up from the aquifer, millions of gallons at the Barton Stacey pumping station.' Jeff saw Alf Harper's weed, upstream of Middleton, in March 1989. 'There was a good growth and then it died off suddenly.'

He is also concerned about run-off from the A303 road, below which he has 1½ miles of water. Above the road he cut his weed in June, July and August. Below the road only in June 'after that it didn't grow'. Poachers are another problem, sometimes hand lining for his fish off the bridges.

Artificial flies came next. His favourite is the Greenwell's Glory. 'You can catch trout any time you like on that fly. Hackled or winged. I like the winged best, but tie more hackled because they're easier. Fly choice goes back to the same old story. There's two types of fly: one to take fish and the other to catch fishermen.' Jeff also favours the Houghton Ruby and Lunn's Particular, and in the late summer a Caperer which, he says, will take fish anywhere on the river. Nymphs are permitted after the June weed cut: the Pheasant Tail is good, and, for bulgers, a Stuart Canham shrimp.

I asked about the size of fly. 'No. 14. The only time you can use a big fly is early on in the season. After the mayfly you must go down to No.

14, but if you go any smaller you are asking for trouble if you get into a big fish where there is weed.'

We went out onto the balcony again.

'Look down at that eddy in the evening. Trout congregate there and millions of Caenis come down. The trout just sit there, on the fin, rising and sinking back, rising and sinking again, opening their mouths, shovelling them in. I can dress a Caenis which will take them. No. 16. I would like to go smaller but I daren't. I've seen so many over the river at the bottom of our garden that it was like a white mist. My fly has white wings, white thorax, white tail and a black head – just a turn of peacock herl.'

We walked up the river. In places the waterway is too wide and too shallow. To improve the depth and flow the width of the river is being reduced by mechanical means. Loads of chalk are brought to be dropped in by a JCB to extend the bank. In addition, if there is a hard river bed, he employs a 17-ton caterpillar tractor which works in the water, pushing the bed towards the banks to narrow and deepen the channel. The necessity to do these things is evidence that water flows are reducing, and I mentioned that Fred Kemp, at Whitchurch, was solving the same problem by the same method. Care must be taken when altering banks, for the changed direction of flow may result in a washed-out opposite bank. Capt. Wills devised a system to test the likely result, tying down bundles of sticks in the selected area. If the change is desirable the extension is permanently chalked over. Islands may be formed in the same manner, to create fast channels on either side.

The estate has purchased an all-terrain-vehicle for Jeff's use. On this he carries materials to repair bridges, seats and to move his fly boards. He has fly boards tethered to all the bridges. Flies lay their eggs on the boards and can then be transported to other places on the river. The eggs are also beyond the reach of egg-consuming caddis larvae. The boards are taken in during the winter. Another mechical aid is home made: a hedge trimmer bar, with two-stroke engine, mounted on a sledge. With this he cuts the river verges at the end of the season.

Middleton Estate. Lara Bingham views reduction in river width to restore rate of flow.

River Dever

HENRY NICOLL

Henry Nicoll lived at Bullington Manor, Micheldever, from the end of the 19th century until his death in 1923. Elected a magistrate on the Andover County Bench, he took his seat for the first time on 10 July 1896. He became a County Councillor and chairman of the Parish Council of Wonston, a small village on the river Dever, a tributory of the Test. It must have been with mixed feelings on 19 May 1900 that he caused this notice to be published in *The Hampshire Chronicle*:

> To the Electors of the MICHELDEVER DIVISION of the County Council.
> Ladies and Gentlemen
> Mr F. R. Hunt having resigned his seat, a vacancy will shortly occur in this Division.
> I have been asked to come forward as a candidate, and should you do me the honour of electing me I will endeavour to represent you to the best of my ability.

Mixed feelings? Nicoll was a trout fisherman, and the week leading up to the election on 28 May was mayfly time. Imagine canvassing when the hatch came up so thick that train passengers at Micheldever had to brush mayflies from their clothes before entering the carriages. Nicoll was a countryman who fished, farmed and shot, but trout fishing was his main summer recreation. So active a man, busy in public life, must have needed those hours of waterside recuperation. When I imagine him, white-moustached in old age, seated on a bench by the river, I recall the words with which D. J. Watkins-Pitchford introduces *The Fisherman's Bedside Book*: 'The wonder of the world, the beauty and the power, the shapes of things, their colours, lights and shades; these I saw. Look ye also while life lasts.'

Henry Nicoll was not a 'dry fly only' man. The following is an extract from an article he wrote for the January 1916 issue of *Salmon & Trout*:

I only once saw gentles used to catch Hampshire trout, and apologising for such a shocking offence against fishing morals, I would plead that it was done under great provocation, and the offence was committed very many years ago. It happened in this way. The junior captain and I were trying to catch fish, with very poor results. We were not 'senior anglers' in those days, and not at all proud. We worked up the stream one Saturday to a spot known as Giddy Bridge*. . . . Just above the bridge was a pool, through which the current ran sluggishly, and in the pool were quite a lot of good trout. We tried them with each and every fly we possessed, but with no tangible result; they would come up and inspect a large light olive, but nothing we could do would induce them to do more than inspect. . . .

We failed altogether on that Saturday, but on Sunday afternoon we held a council of war on Giddy Bridge [there was no fishing on Sunday in those days]. It was evident that something was required which would induce the trout at the critical moment when he was inspecting the fly to lose his head and forget his usual caution. Something alive appeared to be necessary, and gentles came to our minds. On the Monday morning we consulted the jovial village butcher, but he altogether resented the suggestion that he had any gentles on the premises. I have since learnt that it is not good form for a butcher to admit the possession of this useful but malodorous bait. After a little gossip, however, the butcher said he would go and have a look round, and presently returned with what we wanted. They were disgusting gentles, not the sand-cleaned sort dear to the heart of the bottom-fisher, but just sticky, stinking things, and I have thought since that their very smelliness may have been the cause of our great success. We went to Giddy Bridge, put on a large light olive, and then impaled a kicking gentle. Success came at once, the cautious trout came up to inspect as usual; this live white thing was too much for his caution, and the lure was taken without hesitation. I will not say how many fish we took from the pool, for people are sometimes uncharitable over fishing stories.

*Giddy Bridge – Wonston.

Although he wrote many published articles and letters Nicoll only produced one book under his own name, *Salmon and Other Things.* (1923). However, the most widely read volume associated with Henry Nicoll is the Rev. Richard Durnford's classic *Fishing Diary* which he edited and to which he contributed the introduction.

River Dever

JOHN MERISON – OWNER, BRANSBURY MILL
5 OCTOBER 1989

A MILL ON THIS SITE was recorded in *Domesday Book*. On one wall of the present building are the initials: G.F., E.P., W.E., T.P., and M.B. and the date 1782. Inside the mill, which has been converted to a house, is a superb drawing room with minstrel's gallery. Close to the ceiling, in their original positions, are the pulleys used to lift sacks of corn. Within the walls of the house is the wooden paddle wheel and the mill stream flows beneath the floor. Next to the paddle chamber is the ground-floor bedroom of the owners. Water-logged carpets under the bed are a hazard of the past, for John knows that the Dever's level has dropped about nine inches in the five years he has occupied the house. To counteract the fall in the water depth upstream of the mill they have inserted boards in the mill sluice. No previous owner needed to take this action to retain a sufficient depth to provide cover for trout.

The mill stream is taken off the Dever half a mile above the house. After flowing through the mill the diverted water rejoins the river 200 yards downstream. The upper division is just below the Merisons' top boundary, and the fishing continues for about one mile below the garden. Narrow rustic bridges cross the river; it is a beautiful winding stream. In the water meadows sheep graze, herons fish the river edges and willows bend over the pools. There are two pairs of kingfishers. John is not fond of moorhens: 'They go for the ground birds' nests, the ducks' eggs, they are a nuisance.'

When talking about his fishing management he told me that they had to electric fish the water four years ago because the river had been neglected. The result was the removal of many grayling and 36 pike of which the largest weighed 11 lb. John is not too happy about the effect on fly life of this method of control, on nymphs and caddis larvae. 'It doesn't affect the mayfly. We have a tremendous hatch.' Close to the garden is an old swimming pool into which he puts 4 oz brown trout fingerlings in May for the next year's stocking. At times he purchases takeable trout from the Hungerford trout farm to stock straight into the river. To cover some of the costs of the fishing he lets Tuesday, Wednesday and Thursday to three season rods on each day. Friday to Monday is retained for the house.

It was clear that this delightful stream was desperately short of water. The fall had been going on for some seasons and was not solely due to the 1989 drought. Because of the reduced flows the river silts and more weed grows. The more weed the slower the flow – and so the problems compound. To remove ribbon weed and clear the bed for trout to spawn John wants to harrow the Dever with a team of horses working up the river. He hopes to do this in conjunction with Capt. Andrew Wills 'Who has a fair whack of acres.'

Govett's Estate, Newton Stacey

TERRY SNELGROVE — TROUT-KEEPER
23 OCTOBER 1989

To REACH TERRY'S COTTAGE one drives along a narrow road near Newton Stacey, minding wandering pheasants on the way. I pulled up outside the gate of 'Riverside' as Terry emerged from his front door, thrust his feet into black gum boots and called 'Go in. I'll be back soon.' Off he went with Nigel Powis, his under-keeper.

Inside I looked about: a pine table and comfortable chairs in a warm kitchen. Mrs Snelgrove made me welcome. 'That's Terry's collection of fish-weighing scales' she said, gesturing to gleaming brass spring balances hanging from a beam on the wall. They were Salters, about ten in number, all old and optimistic – up to 120 lb. On top of them rested a telescopic toasting fork. All were polished, cared for, hanging in a row. To their left squatted an old wood-fired Rayburn stove, the heart of the house which need never go out while trees grow in the forest.

Terry had returned. He stood and blocked the entrance; light squeezed around him; a large man. Confident and self-reliant he took me into the sitting room and we exchanged news and views. Anglers, genuine members of the brotherhood, are never short of fishing opinions, news and optimism.

He cares for $8\frac{1}{2}$ miles of bank on the Test and its tributary the Dever, a length of just over four miles of river. Only one bank is fished, the other being left wild to benefit fly and other wildlife.

'I was born in Totton in the New Forest. I always loved the Test and used to swim in it as a boy.' I asked about his career. He told me he had worked through an apprenticeship as a plasterer, followed by a period in the merchant navy. After this he became a steeplejack and lost two fingers from his right hand. 'But I always fished. Always. I used to fish for grayling at Bossington, Fairey's water, and in return, in my holidays, I helped weed cut and shift mud. This job came up and I took it. That was 15 years ago and I've been here ever since.'

42

He considers it a great pity that he has few fish other than trout and grayling. There are some roach. The reason for this absence of variety in the river is that almost all the estates electro-fish. He has never electro-fished at Newton Stacey. 'I don't believe in it. It damages fly nymphs and caddis. I know for a fact, whatever the boffins say, that it kills crayfish. The amount of fly life I have now compared to when I arrived is unbelievable. They come down in clouds. Any grayling I want out of the river – I've got friends who come and coarse fish with barbless hooks. Grayling make good eating.'

I questioned his claim that electro-fishing killed crayfish. 'Years ago when I was a boy I used to swim in the river, at Nursling Mill and such-like. As lads we could go there and catch a hundred crayfish in a couple of hours. Now there are very very few. We used to use the little ones as chub bait. Since I've been here I've seen two natural crayfish in the river; one of those was dead, in the Dever, washed up against the screens. At one time we bred crayfish, big ones, American and Swedish they were, for the table. We had several thousand and a few escaped into the river. I think that was a good thing because crayfish and eels are the dustbins of the river. They eat the dead things; keep the river clean. Soon there'll be no eels; everyone's catching them in eel traps. Today, if fish die, they lie there on the bottom because there's nothing to eat them. People don't like to admit this, but the Test is a pretty diseased river. We've got Furunculosis, UDN, IPN, you name it, we've got it. I feel that the decline in eels and crayfish has contributed to this. Think about roach, dace and chub. I know the dace dimples at the surface, but basically they clean up the river, they're bottom feeders. They are not there now, so who's doing the cleaning?'

On water levels Terry has seen a gradual reduction over the years, with 1989 the worst. 'They pump the water out of the chalk. But I've no problem with sewage pollution from the treatment works at Barton Stacey. They're very good, but you get phosphates from that works and nitrates off the land; pig effluent as well at one time. When they come together in a thick soup you get this vast explosion of weed. Mind you, the pigs have gone now and they're cutting down on the nitrogen. I'm lucky here, I've got water meadows alongside the river, they filter the run-off and are not cultivated; they are topped for thistles, that's all.'

A few salmon reach his water to dig half a dozen redds in November, and a few go on to Jeff Smith's at Longparish. Ten or so years ago they went through the hatches into the Dever, but he hasn't seen them there in recent years. I asked whether, in his experience, large trout will eat salmon fry. 'I don't know about that, but I've seen a big trout eat a duckling. He was swimming about for two or three days with a pair of feet hanging out of his mouth. We have a carrier called the Rainbow Stream; it's about half a mile long, isolated from the river, and just holds rainbows. There I've seen a rainbow take a rat. Mind you, the rainbow weighed about 14 lb! Once I noticed a brown trout with an eel's tail sticking out of its mouth; it hung there for a week.'

We went on to talk about his rods, methods of fishing and stocking. He does not encourage wading. 'The river is not wide. There's no need to wade. On some waters you've got to, but not here.' Govett's is divided into two fisheries. First, there is the Bransbury Common water which is fished by four people. 'That's been going on for years and years, since grand-father Govett's time. They have an arrangement between them, and the water is looked after by my under-keeper, Nigel Powis. Nigel's father works on the river at Laverstoke under Dave Walford. Then there's Newton Stacey fishery which is divided into three beats: the Dever (1 mile); and two beats on the Test ($\frac{1}{2}$ mile each).'

He didn't say a great deal about his fishermen, other than a rod who had clearly made an impression 'I've one who's a hands and knees man. He's dedicated. Jim Hughes makes his own rods and flies. His favourite fly is the Black Gnat, and mine too. I'm a great believer in the old flies: Black Gnat, Caperer, Tups – those kind of flies. Coarse fishermen like to collect floats; fly fishers hoard flies. The more they've got the more they like it. I like my flies winged, they present better, and I use solid Mucilin, not that liquid stuff. Presentation is everything; not so much during the mayfly when you can catch them with anything. A fly must sit up and make pin pricks on the water skin. A No. 18 is good. On my stretch of the river the Caperer will take fish when all else fails; I don't know why. I don't tie flies because so many of my fingers are missing but I repair cane rods. I do all the cane rods round here. I've got a Hardy of my own, a Hololite with three tops, it's in my shed.'

What changes had he seen over the years? 'Years ago, when I first came here, I worked for Mr Govett's mother. In those days it was "guests only". It is only recently that we have become a commercial fishery. The guests came down for the first time as regular as clockwork on 27 May, each year, for the mayfly. I'd then see four or five people through the summer before the guests came back in September. In those days I had to keep trout, all browns, up to 9 lb in weight to put in the river. The largest we caught weighed 9 lb 8 oz. It took me a long time, six or seven years, to grow a brown to that size and I would lose some on the way.' The present stocking policy is to buy in 2000 fingerlings annually. There are three stews: for fingerlings, one-year-old trout and the third for two-year-olds. At the end of each season he has a good stock left over of mixed sizes to provide varied stocking for the following year.

Poaching is always a problem on the river. He has his troubles in this direction, some arising from the ill-informed attitude of the public. Two years ago 770 fish of between $\frac{3}{4}$ and $1\frac{1}{2}$ lb were lost in one night from the stews. 'The trouble is that people have still got this romantic idea of poachers, of some little old man going out to catch his dinner. That's just not true. Poaching is an organized big money thing. It cost us £2000 to replace those stolen fish. The men came from Newbury and were caught. We were awarded £600 and they were fined £600, so some of it came back. A policewoman rumbled them at 4 am. Their car was pulling a trailer on which one of the rear lights did not work. She stopped them, smelt fish, and they were caught. It's not poaching; it's stealing. There *is* no poor little old man any more who goes fishing for his dinner.'

We left the cottage to walk across the fields to the river: 'It's the driest year I've known; worse than 1976.' We reached the Dever. 'You see those hatches, six of them, they were opened to flood the water meadows – that gave an early bite of grass in the spring.' The river flowed silently, a pale watery hatched, and blanket weed was everywhere. 'There's never a day on the Dever when fly don't hatch. You see that dead fish? In the old days crayfish would have eaten that, now it'll rot away. Look at that water, it's nine inches lower than usual.'

By the river were vast water pipes with a diameter of about three feet. 'At one time those pipes were brought to carry water across this field, below ground, from the Test to the Dever when that stream got low. The Water Board wouldn't allow it, so we sunk them in the ground to use as snipe butts.'

We reached the trout stews, the beds of which were clear of silt and

glistening with light chalk, stones and gravel. Athletic trout of all sizes up
to 6 lb swirled. Some spawn on these ideal beds and thus lose some condition
which is rapidly regained on daily feeds of trout pellets. Many thick stemmed
nettles grew about the pens and up the wire netting 'One thing poachers
don't like is being stung, and the nettles provide shade in the summer.'
On we went, down the Dever. 'We had a bittern in there last year,' said
Terry, indicating a willow plantation. 'They did a pheasant drive, and this
bittern came out. There are dozens of water rails. Greylag geese nest here;
we've a flock of them and Canadas too, I've even seen a snow goose. We
had a pair of short-eared owls, and as for warblers, lots, and one autumn
an osprey came by on migration.' In the earth held by the roots of the butt
of a large tree blown over in the 1987 gales I saw the holes of a kingfisher's
nest: two holes, one for 1988 and the 1989 site with white droppings hanging, like a beard, below the opening.

The Dever winds, there are many bends, deep holes and rushing shallows. 'This is the first year I've seen blanket weed as bad as this; silt, too. But if we have a good rain, cut the weed and there is a good flow we'll see off the silt. Look at that grayling. Beautiful isn't he? Largest grayling we've had here, taken out, was 2 lb 14 oz. I like to see them in the river. See those trout? They've started to spawn. By the end of November there will be 20 or 30 pairs here and the bed of the river will look as though you have been over it with a shovel.' A shoal of grayling dashed by. 'Look at them. They're beautiful. They've got a place in the river. So have roach and dace. There they go. See them? If people go on the way they're going what will be left? Shooting this and shooting that.'

There was much weed in the river and rushes along the banks. Terry had been off work for eight months after dropping a 2 cwt blacksmith's anvil on his leg, shattering the bones. 'I wanted the anvil to work on, to set the angle of my scythe. All scythes are set individually for a man. I couldn't stand it in hospital after being on the river each day.'

Near the junction of the Test and the Dever is the fishing hut, thatched and lonely, in a glade called the Fish Gardens where there are old disused stews. The record book in the hut gave total catches:

1984	303
1985	478
1986	509
1987	552
1988	612
1989	452

There was a note in the book below the entry of 24 July 1985:

Heller 3, $2\frac{3}{4}$, $4\frac{1}{4}$, 2 Dever
    ,,   guest 8 lb, $6\frac{1}{2}$ lb, 4 lb, $3\frac{1}{2}$ lb Beat 2.

and a comment below this by another rod whose identity is discernible from the writing:

I HOPE YOU DON'T INVITE HIM AGAIN

Wherwell, Countess of Brecknock's Estate

BILL HAWKINS — TROUT-KEEPER
18 JANUARY AND 5 JULY 1989

ON A CARRIER OF THE TEST, close to the Chilbolton/Wherwell road, a man cut weed while wading downstream in chest waders. Pipe in mouth, shoulders bowed, watched by two black labradors seated on the bank in the evening sun, he swung his Turk scythe. That was my first sight of Bill.

I crossed the field to his back and, warned by the sharp barks of his retrievers, he turned, climbed out and queried my presence. We talked. 'Weed is always cut working downstream,' he explained while sharpening the long curved blade of the scythe on a whetstone, 'the flow carries the cut weed away. There are several cuts in the fishing season, but in the winter I clear the river bed and the current washes away the mud.' The carrier was not deep, perhaps one or two feet, and the bed, clear when the silt had whirled away, was of small stones and gravel. Trout spawn here and, occasionally, salmon. A few pale olives drifted by on the warm breeze. 'I caught two grayling on a nymph in the second week of January. Fine firm fish they were. The winter is their time.' He put the whetstone back in his pocket and, since dusk would soon fall, knocked out his pipe and set about finishing the work.

We did not meet again until July during the fishing season. Stripped to the waist in the afternoon heat Bill was trimming the verges with a sickle. I felt he did not have much time for machines, noise and petrol fumes, preferring traditional methods of keeping his river in trim. We sat on the grass in the sun as swallows hawked flies and a woodpigeon cooed sleepily. 'I came to the river 20 years ago next December from the coal mines of

OPPOSITE *Famous Test trout flies (tied and photographed by Peter Gathercole)*: TOP ROW *Lunn's Particular; Caperer;* CENTRE *Houghton Ruby;* MIDDLE ROW *Iron Blue; Little Marryat;* CENTRE *Halford May Fly;* BOTTOM ROW *Adams (an American interloper); Gold-ribbed Hare's Ear.*

48

Yorkshire. I worked underground for 18 years, mainly on the coal face.' Always he thought of an outside life, river-keeping, working on a shoot or in some other country pursuit. He fished in his spare time on the river Witham in Lincolnshire for bream, roach and pike. 'Once you get the fishing bug – that's it.'

Then came the breakthrough. He saw an advertisement for a river-keeper on the Test, applied, and was granted an interview. To his initial dismay he found that another young miner from the same pit had been seen the day before. 'But I got the job,' he said, sad but satisfied, because the earlier applicant, Jeff Smith, was a friend.

For 18 months Bill worked under the supervision of Paul O'Toole who then died. Lady Brecknock* ('She's a good boss') let Bill continue. For six months he worked on his own under the direction of Mick Lunn. 'Anything I wanted to know, I just rang him up.' At the end of the six months it was agreed that Jeff Smith should come down from Yorkshire to join him as under-keeper. Between them they looked after the river for 17 years. Jeff is now head keeper to Capt. Andrew Wills at Middleton (page 32).

The estate fishing season starts on 1 May and closes on 30 September for day rods, and on 10 October for the regular rods. Bill has five miles of water on the main river and carriers, divided into eight beats. The beats are fished on a rotation basis by 11 season rods and additional day rods.

No rainbows are stocked, but 'We have rainbows in the river – escapees.' Each April he buys 2000 brown trout fry from Mick Lunn. He feeds them on for two years and enters them at about 2 lb in three stockings; April, June and early August. As we spoke, his stock consisted of fingerlings from the November 1988 stripping, yearlings and two-year olds. He likes to stock after each weed cut.

The weed cutting is a major work, carried out in those periods specified each season for the whole river by the Test and Itchen Fishing Association. He has three methods: Turk scythe, pole scythe and the link scythe. This year his water cleared in late June after that month's cut. It clears a little later each season. Ten years back it was like gin by March or April. The

*Marjorie, Countess of Brecknock died, aged 89, in August 1989.

OPPOSITE *Fullerton Mill.*

water is not as clear and pure as it was in his early years.

He hoped there would be a thunderstorm that evening, as forecast, for eels would then run down-river at once. There had been a new moon two days before and, as eels run on the darkest nights, there would be one more week of trapping on the grid before the waxing moon made the nights too light. He would then await the darkness between full moons for the second run of the season. His eels start to migrate in June. Lower down the river, at Houghton and Compton, they start in July. He has two eel traps and keeps his catch in a storage box before taking them down to Mick Lunn's where all the keepers meet about four times a year in the morning. A man comes down from London 'who has his own tattie and eel shop. He keeps them alive in the back.'

Fly life is abundant: little gnats, iron blues, blue-winged olive, hawthorn and the mayfly. The mayfly was earlier by two weeks in 1989; usually the hatch begins during the third week of the month. 'I remember well, years ago, seeing the first mayfly on 4 May. That day Leeds, the football team I support, was playing in the Cup Final – and lost. I'll never forget that day.' He mused for a moment, footballs and goal posts before his eyes, then, jerking back to the present 'Sedge fly have been active since mid-June, the brown sedge, in the evening, dancing.' Bill likes the iron blue best. 'There was an old gentleman came here, years ago, and from 1 May to the last day of September, no matter what fly was on the water, he always fished with the Iron Blue. No. 16 or No. 18 hook, he used. I was with him one day and there were mayfly coming down. Mayfly after mayfly. He said "Well, Hawkins, we'll have to change it to the mayfly. You tie on the fly." I said "Hang on, I'll have to get my spectacles." He was a nice old boy.'

I asked him about wild spawning. His trout redd in November; salmon in December. 'They make a mess of the river bed, in the shallows.' Bill does not hold it against them for disturbing his water. 'Well, I think if he's come this far he's done very well, let him keep going, good luck to him.' This tolerant attitude contrasts with the opinion expressed in 1934 by C. Ernest Pain in his book *Fifty Years on the Test*. In Chapter 11, Salmon as Vermin, he writes:

'It has been claimed that, as salmon do not feed in fresh water, the presence of the large fish cannot harm trout fishing. But *parr* feed in fresh water; they do nothing else but feed – in fact, except for an occasional light interlude spent annoying the trout angler by chewing his flies – the voracious little beggars.'

He told me of an unusual experience which he hopes will never be repeated! 'One January me and young Jeff were working together on the Dublin carrier. The coldest winter I can remember. I stumbled in my thigh boots and fell in up to my neck. I said to Jeff "Get the Land Rover. Take me home." So he got the Land Rover and I sat there, shivering, in a pool of water. I said "You might as well laugh. Get it over." So he had a good laugh. Then I went home, stripped, threw me clothes outside, had a good drink of whisky and a cup of coffee. I went outside and all me clothes was frozen stiff. I stood them up outside against the door.'

Original Wherwell Estate trout hatchery. Built in 1930 by Cecil Hill's father (of Compton). Now disused.

Chilbolton

REV. RICHARD DURNFORD

THE LIVING OF CHILBOLTON was for years a sinecure for the 18th century deans and prebendaries of Winchester Cathedral who were able to enjoy fishing on the Test while leaving the real work of the parish to curates. It appears from the parish records that there had been no full time rector for many years prior to the appointment of Richard Durnford, LL.B., in 1806, in response to complaints from parishioners.

Mr Durnford fortunately had private means with which to augment the £50 per annum stipend which came with the job. No doubt his acceptance of the position was influenced by free occupation of the rectory, and fishing in the rivers Test and Anton. His duties cannot have been time-consuming for during his years of office he kept a detailed fishing diary, which was edited by Henry Nicoll in 1911 (page 37). Many of the entries have a familiar ring.

Untimely weed cutting caused anglers in those days the same annoyance as now, and there is a feeling reference, on 20 May, 1817, to 'that minute gnat which is so very vexatious to the fisherman.' The rising fish, he notes, 'would not take the artificial fly though they rose and took the gnat under the very line. At this season very little is to be done except with a minnow, or in evening fishing when the thermometer is at 60°.'

From the *Diary* it is also clear that many of the Rev. Durnford's fish were taken with the natural fly, especially in mayfly time. He also used the blow-line, carefully recording the force of the wind each day. When there was no wind he would often use the cross-line [one person on each side of the river with a fly suspended mid-stream below a cross line held up by a rod at each end].

The following entry is typical:

'Monday, June 12, 1809. – Wind S.S.W., sufficient. The sun was very bright until about 11 a.m. At twelve began in the boat on the Broad at West Down. The fly rose partially at that time and continued to rise till past seven o'clock. About four o'clock it was very strong, and the fish rose well upon the shallow near Cow River, but were scarcely to be taken in the clear and shallow water. The fish were principally caught among the weeds. The atmosphere was cloudy towards the afternoon, and some slight showers of rain passed along:

	No.	lb	oz
DURNFORD, IN THE BOAT	22	33	12
PENROSE, ON SHORE	4	6	12
	26	40	8'

Today, from time to time, one hooks a swift when casting the mayfly. The birds fall in the river, brought up short by the line, and often die after the shock of immersion. Blow lining increased this hazard. On 14 June 1816 Durnford recorded: 'Three swifts hooked themselves as the N.F. [natural fly] was floating in the wind; the force these animals exert in their stout and short claws is very great, and causes much pain when they grasp the finger.'

That the blow line depended upon wind to carry out the fly is apparent from the care with which the wind's strength is recorded. Durnford's categories were: sufficient, quite sufficient, strong, whistling and very violent.

'23 May, 1811, wind W.S.W., quite sufficient, sun brighter. Began at Garrison at 12 o'clock. No fly on the water, fish quiet. Tried several kinds of natural flies, Father Long-legs and such others as could be caught. Observed a fish come several times to a Father Long-legs but would not take it. Tried him with a Blue-bottle, which he took immediately. Caught also another fish with the same kind of fly, and hooked a third – all in very shallow water.'

The *Diary* also shows the regularity of his fishing. In the ten years covered by his *Diary*, Durnford's season usually began in March, and never earlier than the 25th. The mayfly weeks had his full attention, and there is no entry later than 1 July.

Rivers Anton and Test, Fullerton

MAJOR CHARLES LIDDELL
31 AUGUST 1989

Between 1900 and 1910 Major Liddell's great uncle bought three farms: Cottonworth, Westover Farm and Fullerton Manor. With them came double bank fishing on the Anton from its junction with the Test almost to Goodworth Clatford. A short section at the top of the water was single bank. In addition, with the farms, went the right bank of the Test upstream of the Anton junction for about one mile, where the river flows in a loop to the east and then continues south. Major Liddell took over these farms in 1960.

The fishing is kept in hand and rods are let. Stocking is of brown trout which are purchased from Mick Lunn at weights up to 4 lb. This stocking takes place about once a month, straight into the river. No trout are fed on in stews, but after the end of the fishing season several hundred yearlings are introduced from the stripping of the previous autumn.

Major Liddell himself fishes about once a week, preferring dry fly to nymph, although both are allowed. He finds the nymph more difficult.

He has not noticed any reduction in the quality of the water or an increase in weed growth, but feels there is a problem arising in the reduction of water flows. This reduction he cannot quantify due to lack of records. Indeed, there seemed to be remarkably little information on this stretch of the river, but I discovered the following extract from *Fifty Years on the Test* by C. Ernest Pain (published in 1934):

Just below Testcombe the Test is joined by the Anton, which rises above Andover, and at Upper Clatford the Anna brook flows into it. Here there was a fishing club formed by Mr Fowle and in this water Francis Francis often fished. The club water extended to Lower Clatford and held a great number of trout. After the club was broken up, the water was rented by Mr Cuthbert, who one day caught twenty-four

56

trout with wet flies fished downstream amidst heavy falls of snow. How often have I seen a good hatch of Winter Duns in a snowstorm in midwinter. The Anton holds a great number of fish of about one and and a quarter pounds, with of course some running larger, and is a most delightful stream.

I am indebted to Mrs Liddell who, before I left Fullerton Grange gave me the opportunity to amplify this thin store of information on the Anton, for it was she who gave me Douglas Lickman's address, saying 'Write to him. He may still be alive. He's the son of an old keeper, Bill Lickman, whom we employed for 50 years.'

Douglas had died in 1981, but I was able to trace Bill's grandson to Eastleigh. Michael Lickman produced a family photograph album, copies of the magazines *Shooting Times* for 1957 and *Hampshire* for 1969 relevant to his grandfather, and some photographs handed down from Dr Barton, author of *Pictures of the Chalk Streams* who died in 1953, aged 89.

Leckford Estate. Robert Goldsworthy holds a brood trout.

Rivers Anton and Test

WILLIAM LICKMAN — TROUT-KEEPER 1881 TO 1969

If you leave the Andover to Stockbridge road at Fullerton, cross the Anton by the bridge adjacent to Fullerton Mill, on the right you will see Vine Cottage, Bill Lickman's home, thatched, thick-walled and facing the river. There he and his wife Elizabeth brought up their son Douglas. Later the Lickmans moved to one of the semi-detached cottages closer to Fullerton Grange. Douglas did not follow his father as a river-keeper.

Fullerton. A dovecot converted to a World War 2 pill box.

Bill served in the Great War as a sharpshooter in the Royal Hampshire Regiment and then returned to the river. His underkeeper was Joe Smith who lived in Fullerton Mill before he retired to Cottonworth. Joe, who died in 1981 at the age of 69, was born at Collingbourne Ducis and took over care of the river on the death of Bill Lickman. I asked Michael for memories of Joe: 'When Bill and Joe were weed cutting from the bank, Joe sat on a wasp's nest. He had to run across the field from the nest, take off his trousers and jump into the river,' and of his grandfather: 'Bill once saved a fisherman from a bull. Below Fullerton Mill there is a field on the left which backed on to "The Seven Stars" (a public house now re-named "The Mayfly"). The farmer had a fierce bull in this field and this animal was making a bee-line for the fisherman who was unaware of his peril. Bill ran across and swept the angler and himself into the river.' Bill is buried in the churchyard of St Mary-the-Less, Chilbolton, behind the church, in the far corner, looking down the valley.

Bill Lickman with his son Douglas at Vine Cottage, Fullerton.

Leckford and Longstock

LECKFORD AND LONGSTOCK FISHING CLUBS

Probably the best source of information about the origins of the Long-stock Club is *The Trout* written by the Marquess of Granby and published in 1898. I include the following extract for the benefit of those readers without access to this now quite rare book.

'The Longstock Club is the same as the old Leckford Club . . . . The Club records date from 1798, and from then till now every fish caught has been duly weighed, and the book kept in perfect order.

'It is a fact that for more reasons than one, the "catch" deteriorated from 1850 to 1870, compared with that at the commencement of the century; when over 400 fish were caught during one mayfly season in the water below Testcombe Bridge to within three-quarters of a mile of Stockbridge . . . . Whether to the clearness of the water, or the higher education of the fish, can be attributed the diminution of the size of the bags, it is impossible to say. But it is probable that with the increased number of sportsmen almost every trout has been either "pricked", or hooked and returned to the river as not "sizeable."

'Possibly the "patchiness" of the Mayfly may have had something to do with this, but at any rate we are now told that 100 to 150 fish during a whole season, Mayfly time included, may be considered a satisfactory number: 9 to 13 trout in a day to one rod being sometimes the red-letter bag of the season. These fish would average 2 lb in weight. As to big fish of 5 lb and upwards – 5 lb 8 oz being the largest killed – they amount to a dozen in 100 years. Four-pound fish have been more numerous possibly amounting to a hundred in the same period. The 10,000 or 11,000 trout caught average within a fraction of 2 lb, so that it is clear fish of 2 and 3 lb must be the most numerous.

'Till about the year 1868 the only flies used were large ones, tied on

No. 8 hooks, Mayflies and moths being the most common artificial ones. Early in the century the "blow line" was introduced from Ireland, the natural fly on a No. 8 hook being used. For this purpose a hollow cane rod of some 24 feet, or even one made of deal, was the general weapon. Nowadays such a proceeding is hardly ever heard of in English rivers. About the year 1860 the tiny "dry" artifical small gnat, and the 10 or 11 foot rod, which had previously come into use on other smaller streams in England, became the customary system of fishing the Test. . . .

'The Stockbridge Club I believe to have been founded by Hampshire men. Not so the Leckford, now the Longstock Club. This was created by gentlemen from Northumberland, who came down solely for the Mayfly season; the Rev. Ogle being the absolute originator, and the first Secretary.

'At that time Ogles, Sheridans, and the Duke of Argyll figure among the members of the Club. A little later came more Sheridans: while Abercorns, Streatfields, Bathursts and many others have up to these times filled the roll of members. . . . In truth it must have been no light or easy matter, at the end of the last century [i.e. the 1790s] to travel the whole way from Northumberland to Hampshire; and men must have been keen sportsmen indeed to undertake such a journey for the sake of a week or ten days' fishing, even though it were the Mayfly time. . . .

'What a difference there is nowadays! The 9.15 a.m. train from Waterloo will take you to Stockbridge, or anywhere in those parts, in time to allow you to begin fishing by 12.30, or thereabouts, and to return to London the same evening.'

1827 Fire Insurance Policy of thatched fishing cottage in Leckford occupied by 'Gentleman belonging to the Leckford Fishing Club'.

Leckford and Longstock

DAVID OWEN — MD LECKFORD ESTATE
21 SEPTEMBER 1989

DAVID OWEN IS THE PRESENT Managing Director of Leckford Estate, a branch of the John Lewis Partnership. Knowing that Vikings had sailed up the Test to just above Stockbridge, I had written to ask David if he had any evidence on the estate of their presence. We met at the estate office, then drove to Longstock. We crossed a field, pressed our way through thick undergrowth and willows and there, some distance from the river was a depression. It was the Viking dockyard, now a banked up area about 75 yards by 100 yards. In their day, AD 800 to 1000, the river ran alongside the banking over which they must have hauled their longships for repair in the dry-dock.

The yard is within a stone's throw of the old route of invader and defender which ran between Danebury and Woolbury, Danebury being on the Longstock side and Woolbury on the Leckford side of the river. There was a ford where the present bridge crosses the river at Longstock and the track is straight as an arrow between these two places. The route comes down the present Church Road in Longstock, crosses the river, and then continues on the Leckford side over the golf course and straight on to the Woolbury encampment. Undoubtedly there were battles in the Longstock area. 'One or two of us of Celtic origin have heard tramping feet in the village. White Shape Bridge is haunted – hence the name; it was erected when the canal was built. People see peculiar things there at night, and I have felt something up here, presences, it is quite interesting.'

David told me that one of his gardeners, 'An intelligent, well read man,' found peculiar plants in the area. It was the gardener's opinion that they only grew on battlefields – they are also found at Naseby.

On the Leckford Estate is a field known as Red Verlyn; verlyn being a Norse measurement from which, possibly, furlong is derived. In Longstock are Furlong Cottages.

Before we parted David reminisced on Ernie Mott, the old head river-keeper, long dead, under whose care I had spent my first day on the river in about 1952. 'Ernie was the world's supreme optimist. He was determined to keep his rods in good heart and working hard. He used to say, when one had experienced a disappointing evening "Don't forget, Sir, they all eventually make a mistake." My son, Mark, as a young boy, once caught a trout of over 7 lb. We took it up to Ernie's cottage opposite The Peat Spade. Young Mark stood in front of Ernie with this huge trout cradled in his arms, overlapping at each end. Ernie asked if he would like it set up. Mark thought for a moment and then said "No thank you Mr Mott. I'll wait until I catch a larger one".'

'The Seven Stars Inn', Fullerton c 1920. Now renamed 'The May Fly'.

Leckford and Longstock

MAURICE JONES — RETIRED MANAGING DIRECTOR,
LECKFORD ESTATE.
24 FEBRUARY 1989

Maurice and Isobel Jones entertained me to lunch in The Grange which had at one time been the headquarters of the Longstock Fishing Club founded *c.* 1798. We sat in the drawing room, the original club room, from which one looks over the Test to the east. Upstream is the Leckford trout hatchery; Longstock church is to the north of the house and Leckford church to the north-east. The house had ample bedrooms for the members.

A Cambridge graduate, Maurice was commissioned in the Gunners, captured during the war at Singapore and worked on the railway. On his release he came as assistant to the Leckford Estate manager, Walter Hollis, a respected but rather old-fashioned farmer. Hollis died within 18 months of Maurice's arrival – 'Nothing to do with me!'. Maurice then became Managing Director of Leckford Estate in 1948 and held this position until his retirement in 1980, when he was succeeded by David Owen.

The estate is about 4000 acres, 2000 to the east of the river and 2000 on the Longstock side. The river fishing runs from just north of Stockbridge, where it joins the Houghton Club water, upstream to Fullerton. When Maurice was in control of the estate there were 13 beats, six of which were kept permanently for members of the staff fishing club. The remaining beats were let to various rods: week-end, mid-week, or a whole rod. To begin with they only stocked brown trout. The head-keeper when Maurice joined the estate was Ernie Mott. In the 1950s it became necessary to commercialize the fishing, reduce the days kept for Mr Lewis, and let more rods. But it was found that after a heavy mayfly the fishing went dead in July and the paying rods became a trifle restless at failing to catch fish. Mott then came to Maurice with the suggestion that rainbow trout be introduced at that time, and the stocking became two-thirds brown and one-third rainbow. The management of the river was, of course, in the hands of Mott, Maurice concerning himself with wider ranging matters that bore upon the river. Two of these were dredging and gravel extraction.

In the early 1950s Leckford was threatened with dredging by the River Authority who had already worked up the valley to Fishlake Meadows just above Romsey, by Great Bridge. The Authority was determined to drop the water level by three feet. It had almost been agreed that they would do this as far as Stockbridge, and then continue north of the town. Maurice and the then Chairman of John Lewis, Bernard (now Sir Bernard) Miller, resisted, fought and won, with the result that no dredging took place south of Stockbridge. Whether they will succeed in the battle against gravel extraction in the river valley is a matter of conjecture. 'Years ago Lady Brecknock applied to extract gravel, but the planners turned her down after a public enquiry, partly because the roads were incapable of carrying the gravel lorries.' I asked whether he was willing to be quoted on the present extraction proposal at Dunbridge. He settled himself into his chair by the fire: 'I am perfectly happy to be quoted. I am dead against it, for the whole of the valley floor is on gravel and the valley had been designated an Agronomically Sensitive Area by the EEC. Once they start you will have exactly the same scene as on the Avon – it looks like Passchendaele from the air. The present inquiry is more difficult to resist as the extraction between Awbridge and Dunbridge is for plastering sand, not gravel. This sand is scarce. The County Council wish to let out contracts because of the tremendous house building in the South of England. I know there is sand in other areas.' Permission for the extraction was granted in the summer of 1989.

I asked if there had been reductions in water levels and flows during his time. 'I think so from looking at the levels, particularly in times of drought. On the estate we have two wells, one on each side of the river. From these we pump to the highest points on both farms and we have never been short.'

Water quality is of concern, the colour being rather cloudy due to trout farms and watercress beds. When he first came to Leckford they did not use as much fertilizer on cereals as today. Present strains have stronger straw which will stand more fertilizer and thus give higher yields. I asked about the source of the straw with which they thatch the fishing huts. 'We grow

---

OPPOSITE *Leckford. Replica of line of old fashioned eel pots. Made by Guy Robinson.*

about 20 acres of wheat for combing. The price of the combed thatching straw will equal the value of the wheat.'

There appeared to be an over-abundance of wildlife. '*Far* too many Canada geese and swans, eating *far* too much weed and knocking down *far* too many electric cables.' The roe deer were in trouble too: 'Lots of them. They swim across the river, get into the water garden and eat the plants.'

Maurice responded to my curiosity about the origin of the John Lewis Partnership's interest in Leckford, the river and the farms. 'In 1928 John Spedan Lewis decided that it was not defensible for him, his father and his brother to take out of the business of John Lewis more in dividends than he paid in total wages to his staff. He therefore decided to turn the enterprise into a partnership. The business was valued and put into the hands of trustees who were required to pay him the capital value. Armed with the first two or three repayments he decided to invest in the countryside. After looking at some properties west of London he came to the Test, and bought Leckford Abbas from a family named Ansdell. There then commenced the gathering of a large holding of land, the process continuing until 1939, and including the Harewood Settled Estates. From Harewood came the Grange, 750 acres, many cottages and one mile of fishing. After the war, in 1946, Longstock House, park, 70 acres and a short stretch of the river were added. This was acquired from the Beddington family who bought it from Joshua East who made money supplying horses to the army during the Crimean War. East had two bachelor sons who are buried in a private graveyard between Longstock and Longstock House.'

OPPOSITE *Vine Cottage, Fullerton 1990.*

Leckford. Robert Goldsworthy (left) helps head keeper Guy Robinson strip a brown trout.

Leckford and Longstock

GUY ROBINSON — TROUT-KEEPER
2 FEBRUARY 1989

G<small>UY'S TROUT HATCHERY</small> is a hut, squat, black-planked and thatched. It stands on an island between two streams which steam a thin mist in cold still weather. Dry reeds blew in the wind and pheasants rustled in the undergrowth as I walked up the path between carriers in which trout arrowed in fright. Guy was inside, a rubber apron extending from his chest to just below the tops of his gum boots. With him was Brian Parker, the Bossington head-keeper. In their hands were devices which reminded me of ancient rubber-bulbed motor car horns. Instead of horns, thin glass tubes protruded from the bulbs, and with these the two men sucked atrophied trout eggs from the bottom of water-filled tanks.

The hatchery was built just before the Second World War to increase trout production. The thatched wooden building gives comfort to keepers and protection from the weather. In the 1950s the hatchery had a concrete floor and was a cold and draughty place; this was in the time of Ernie Mott who had shown it to me. He retired in 1969 to be succeeded by Kim Debenham. Guy worked under Kim for 10 years and together they extended the hatchery, adding a wooden section at one end and installing electricity. When Kim died, Guy took over and continued single-handed: he now has an underkeeper, Robert Goldsworthy.

Inside the hatchery are four rectangular troughs for brown trout, there being about 15–20,000 fry in each. If this number is greater than their requirements, and for sale, the excess is released into the side streams. The fry which I saw are those which had been stripped in November 1988. They had taken 45 days to hatch, a period which is almost constant as the water temperature remains throughout the year at a steady 10°C. The source of the reliable flow and temperature was apparent when the door was opened to an adjoining building. Inside are an old water wheel and pump supplemented by a stand-by electric model. These raise water from 20 feet down, at this constant 10°C, to a header tank in the roof. From this tank water is tapped off as required, and constant circulation in cold weather prevents pipes from freezing solid. River water is not used because the temperature varies; in the winter of 1986 it fell to 2°C. The flow may also become turbid. The fish have the best possible start in spring water and stay in the tanks until March. At this time river water is roughly the same temperature as that pumped up from the ground. When parity is reached the fry are transferred outside to stews. Guy encourages a country interest in the education of schoolchildren, parties of whom visit his river and hatchery. Inside, supported at one end of the building at head height, is an aquarium. The occupants of this glass-sided tank are, with the single exception of a mirror carp, the creatures of the river: a lamprey sucking at the glass, dace, roach, pike and a crayfish. Gudgeon, minnows and sticklebacks were hiding in the weed. Many people come to view his work when the estate does a farm tour: Salmon & Trout Association members, farmers, and recently Australian sheep shearers on holiday.

Leckford Estate. The trout hatchery.

The rearing is 75% brown and 25% rainbow trout. The rainbows being brought on in circular tanks which seem to suit them better. The fish in the building on my visit would be stocked in the 1991 season and subsequently. Some might be fed on until 1993 or 1994, by which time a few would have reached 10 lb in weight.

We left the hatchery to walk the river banks, and at once, to the north, came upon a bench beside the water. 'Kim loved to sit there and look up the river', commented Guy. 'The bench was placed there in his memory.' A brass plaque on the seat reads:

> In loving memory of Kim Debenham, head river keeper 1969 to 1986.
> A man who loved the Test.
> Let's stay awhile and here perchance catch fish.

As we walked Guy pointed to a fishing hut: 'We have 16 of those on 16 beats. One rod fishes each beat and there are 11 miles of bank if you include

Leckford Estate. Netting up trout before transportation to Bossington.

the main river and the carriers. By the way, we make those huts ourselves, and have just completed a larger one higher up the valley in which to store our trout food and equipment.'

We talked about the wildlife: there are now no otters. Roe deer feed along the banks at dusk. Brian, who was walking with us, said that he had fallow deer at Bossington. There were many tufted duck about, the drakes prominent with white flanks; tufted are trapped in the winter in collaboration with the RSPB, ringed and released. The reed beds on both sides of the river are home to many warblers.

We ambled on to a line of eel pots made of wire, basket-shaped with the thin end pointing downstream. The line crossed the river, interrupted close to the western side by a thatched wooden hut. 'When I first arrived on the river these were in use but were at once superseded by a trap of metal grids. The estate asked me to make a "mock-up" line of pots to show how the system worked. There are gaps between these pots, as you can see. When in use they were side by side so that the eels could not get through without being caught. The pots closest to the left bank, under our feet, were the most productive for eels always follow the darkest bank. The new

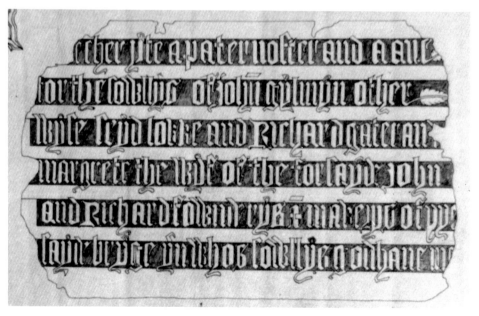

Copper plaque from 15th century 'Test Bridge' at Stockbridge.

74

trap was constructed because these pots were too much work. The end of each pipe had to be blocked with a handful of weed, each had to be lifted to remove the eels, much weed had to be cleared with a long handled hook. We put the catch in wooden boxes which were sent from Fullerton railway station to Billingsgate.'

Eels at Leckford weigh between $\frac{3}{4}$ and 1 lb each, being in the region of 18 inches in length. They run in June and July at the top of the river, through Whitchurch, but lower, at Leckford, Guy takes them in September and October. Since the railway was closed the eels go by road to London in a tanker.

TEST BRIDGE

The first bridge over the river Test is believed to have been built between 1229 and 1245. In the 15th century a bridge was built which carried a copper plaque on which was the inscription:

> Say of your cheryte a
> paternoster and a ave
> for the sowllys of John Gylmyu
> otherwyse seyd Lokke and
> Richard Gater and
> Margrete the wyf
> of the forsayd John and
> Richard fownderys and
> makerys of the sayde
> bryge yn whos sowllys
> God have mercy

In 1799 the bridge was widened and rebuilt at the expense of the County of Southampton. In 1963 the present bridge was constructed.

A. N. Gilbey (left) and William Lunn, honorary secretary and head keeper, The Houghton Club.

The Houghton Fishing Club

OUTLINE OF ITS HISTORY

T HE HISTORY OF THE HOUGHTON FISHING CLUB has been twice recorded. Sir Herbert Maxwell edited the *Chronicles* from the foundation year 1822 to 1908. The *Further Chronicles,* of 1908 to 1931, were edited by R. P. Page in 1932. The Club Centenary celebrations of 7 June 1922 were widely reported. Many thousands of words about the Club have thus been published, and scenes drawn, painted or photographed. To attempt to compress these accounts into a few thousand words, to fit the compass of this general survey of the river, would be an effort doomed to failure. At the same time, the *Chronicles* provide a fascinating source of information. To turn away entirely from those scenes of yesterday would be unforgivable, and the book would be incomplete. What follows is a brief look at the Club's past, a salute to one of its best-known anglers, an account of its Centenary celebrations and the Club as it is today.

From the Introduction by Sir Herbert Maxwell to the *Chronicles*.

The Houghton Fishing Club was founded in June 1822, after the manner described in the following letter written to Mr Martin T. Smith by the Rev. Canon F. Beadon at the age of 88, he being still a member of the Club:

"N. Stoneham, 7th June 1865 – I am very happy to hear from you and will give you whatever information I can furnish respecting our Club.

I will begin with a circumstance which may account for some little mistake regarding the founders.

Poor Barnard and I had been fishing, as visitors, at Longstock, and on our way back we learned from the landlord of the hotel (at Stockbridge) that the fishery would be let. After a little correspondence with King, the landlord, we secured the water – that is, Barnard and myself. Finding that Popham occasionally fished at Houghton, and knowing him to be my old friend, we immediately after offered him the opportunity of joining us, an offer he accepted; we then added other members.

Now I must add – previous to this engagement of our water, I had had an offer from my friend, old Sir Charles Rich, to join the Longstock Club . . . and I left the Houghton Club for my previous engagement; and, after four or five years, when, owing to the present Edward's coming of age, the Longstock Club terminated, myself, Snow, Jarrett, and Sir H. Vivian were received into our present excellent Club. . . ."

The Longstock Club referred to by Canon Beadon had been formed in 1809, when it consisted of five members. After it had been dissolved in 1827, its members were elected to the Houghton Club.

'The founding members of the Houghton Club in 1822 were: the Rev. F. Beadon, Edward Barnard, William Beckford, the Rev. Henry Dampier, Henry Warburton, MP, Richard Penn, the Rev. William Garrett, Sir James Gardiner, Bart., Charles Taylor, MP, Sir Charles Blois, Bart., Francis Popham, Francis L. Beckford, Jr., Colonel Walhouse.'

Maxwell comments on the methods of fishing:

'Considering the complete revolution which has taken place in chalk-stream fishing since Canon Beadon and Edward Barnard first took up their quarters at Stockbridge, one would have expected at least passing reference to such an event as the first use of the dry fly. The old manner was twofold – either to fish down-stream with two flies of a bulk and build that would send every sane twentieth-century trout within sight to the nearest shelter, or to impale a natural fly – grannom, Mayfly or caperer – on the hook and to present it by "blowing" – that is, to let it float before the wind at the end of a line of floss silk and alight in as natural a way as possible on the water. To do so, of course, required a favouring wind, neither too much nor too little . . . . The invention of floating flies rendered the trout-fisher, if not independent of wind, far less dependent on it, and wholly indifferent to calm.'

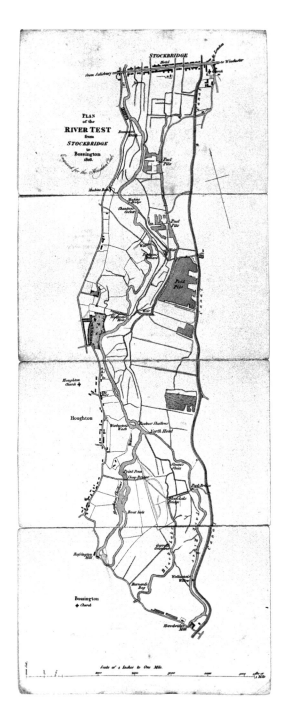

*Plan of the River Test from
Stockbridge to Bossington.
Engraved for The Houghton Club,
1826.*

Between 1874 and 1893 the Club lost, regained and acquired waters. A limited company, the Stockbridge Fishery Association Ltd, was formed to simplify the finances. Subscriptions increased over the years, from £10 in 1822 to £60 in 1893. In 1824 an entrance fee of £5 was imposed, and this rose to £10 in 1827. The number of members increased from 12 at formation to 16 in 1835.

These entries in the *Houghton Chronicles* give a flavour of the fishing its members enjoyed until the turn of the century.

27 June 1830. A letter from Elton (keeper) Stockbridge.

> Sir, I Rite To in Farmyu that this Last Weicke wee Have Been Trubeld very Much with Porchars and wee Watch them very Narely on Sunday mourning A Bout 7 o Cloack Charles Faithfull Maken (?) & Mee cought Joseph Larence & John Tubb a Dradgeing the Water att the Sheep Bridge wee Toock the Dradge Nett From them & thar Great Sticks wee ar going To Have them To Mr. Penbeel (?) To morrow Morning
> Sir wee Remaine your Survents
> John & Charles Elton

3 June 1831. A stoutish gentleman was observed at the angle of the carrier below Sloane's Sluice busily engaged for an hour and a half, after an unusual bustle between him and his attendant. The first surmise of the distant observer was that he had captured a Monster. He was, however, subsequently seen washing and drying some of his undergarments. At last he proceeded slowly towards the Tent, covered with his waterproof cloak; and, on his arrival, stated that he had tumbled in, and was obliged to dry his clothes. The party were bound to believe that this was the *only accident* that had happened. At all events, he dined this day without certain *inexpressible conveniences* which custom sanctions and decency enjoins.

1834 – Origin of grayling in the Test

'About the year 1816 Mr Tate and Mr Snow of Longstock sent John Haines their fisherman to Heron Court to fetch 25 brace of grayling given to them by Lord Malmesbury. Haines brought the fish in a water-cart, and rested them in the miller's trunk at Romsey. One fish only died, and the survivors were put into the River Test at Longstock. They were small, not more than 3 or 4 oz each.'

1834. From the ledger of this period it appears that the rent paid for the waters leased by the club was as follows:

WICKHAM'S	£80
MARSH COURT	25
COOPER'S MEAD	10
PEAT PITS	7
CORPORATION WATER	5
ATWOOD'S, ETC.	8
	£135

The wages of three keepers amounted to £53, 6s., Charles Elton receiving 14s. a week, Faithfull and J. Elton 3s. 6d. and 3s. a week respectively. It is difficult to understand these very low wages except in the nature of a retaining fee, the keepers being remunerated by the anglers on whom they attended.

Other expenses and sundries raised the total disbursement for the year to £242. 6s., to meet which the subscription of the 16 members was raised from £10 to £15 per annum.

5 January 1838. Hang the fishing! Mr. Penn began the New Year by catching one jack 6 lb. He afterwards fell into a ditch.

23 April 1844. Mr Jervoise caught a jack in the Peat Pits on a large fly with large eyes. Mr Penn supposes this engine to be furnished with these prominent orbs so that something may be at hand to be damned in case of ill success.

1 January 1846. James Faithfull and James Harris entered upon office as joint keepers.

There were caught in the Club waters in 1846—
99 Trout weighing 201 lb 14 oz; average 2 lb $\frac{2}{3}$ oz.
73 Grayling weighing 129 lb 13 oz; average 1 lb 11 oz.
Four trout and four grayling were taken of 3 lb and upwards; largest fish, a grayling of 3 lb 6 oz.
In the weir were taken eels weighing 1511 lb, and the keepers took 345 jack weighing 360$\frac{1}{2}$ lb.

15 March 1848. Lord Gage down to fish the peat Pits, and on 16th and 17th caught 14 jack weighing 83 lb 9 oz with a small red fly, ribbed yellow and gold.

13 July 1848. This evening four eels were seen at the edge of a weed in the castaway river, taking small gnats on the surface of the water.

23 April 1850. During the last three days the weathercock on the Town Hall has pointed west, whereas any credulous gentleman thereby tempted to the waterside is met by a cutting nor'-easter. It is to be hoped that the borough authorities will *not* repair the error before the Mayfly season, so that anglers may at least take their breakfast in the pleasing expectation of a fine fishing day.

2 June 1860. A hurricane from S.W. The gale, after loosening some of the ropes of the tent, upsetting all the chairs and breaking some bottles, completely wrecked the tent, which was taken down.

30 May 1865. Tent blown down in the night. A great rise of fish early in the evening, but before it was dark enough to deceive them.

1867. Written by Canon Beadon, at the age of 89, in acknowledgement of a present of trout:

No better trout a man could feed on
Than those you sent to Canon Beadon;
Firm was their flesh, and scarce – I think –
Was ever pretty face so pink.

TOP *A. N. Gilbey, Lord Moreton, D. Meinertzhagen, R. Smith, R. D. Balfour, Houghton Club Dining Tent.* BELOW *The first fire engine in Stockbridge, 1897. Presented to the town as a memorial to the Diamond Jubilee of Queen Victoria. Note onlooker in the window of The Houghton Club.*

1 March 1870. This day being, as he supposes, Shrove Tuesday, Lord Ducie would invite attention to the hostess's pancakes, with which he was regaled at dinner. They were of a size, quality, and consistency not often seen in these days of retrenchment. Large and satisfying, they were much like a folded railway rug in everything but flavour; but, withal, not to be despised.

19 June 1876. Col. Wigram saw a rat swimming, threw at him and hooked him by near hind foot and landed him.
There were caught in the Club waters in the year 1876:

80 TROUT WEIGHING	157 lb	7 oz
2 GRAYLING WEIGHING	3 lb	8 oz
	160 lb	15 oz

Average weight of trout 1lb $13\frac{1}{4}$ oz

1887. An otter was killed by Lunn at North Head. [This is Lunn's first year as head keeper.]

26 April 1888. Every member of the Club will hear with sincere regret of the death today of James Faithfull. Born in 1816, he entered our service in January 1845, and, after being associated with us in our palmiest days for 42 years, he retired on 1st January 1887, on a well earned pension, which he only lived 15 months to enjoy. He was an accurate observer of nature, had a marvellous eye for a rising fish, and a perfect knowledge of every detail of his craft. His name was his character.

17 February 1893. 700 two-year-old trout arrived from Norwich, of which 500 were the gift of Lord Penryn and Mr Martin Smith. They were put into the nursery at Stockbridge. Our old tent was bought in 1861 for £30 6s. Such care has Harris taken of it that £11 3s. 2d. has sufficed to put it in perfect repair, and it is pronounced almost as good as new.

28 May 1894. – *Conversation overheard.*
Lord Penryn (to Waiter): 'What has Mr Norman caught?' Waiter: 'The

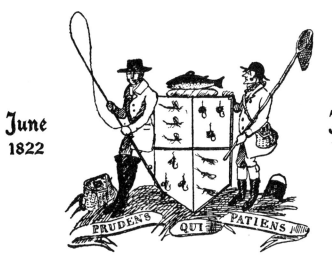

The Centenary of

June 1822

June 1922

PRUDENS QUI PATIENS

The Houghton Club

at

Claridge's Hotel.

—

7th June 1922.

The Centenary celebrations of The Houghton Club at Claridge's Hotel, 7th June 1922.

4.5, my Lord.' Lord Penryn: 'What! four or five?' Waiter: 'No, my lord; the 4.5 train.'

4 May 1899. Mr Norman arrived to dinner, bringing with him the enormous fish, $11\frac{1}{2}$ lb, which he killed last year, has had set up, and now presents to the Club.

1902. Telegraph is being expanded down to Houghton.

1904. The keepers killed during the year 635 pike.

29 May 1906. Mr A. N. Gilbey killed 12 trout weighing 25 lb 1 oz, and on the 30th 13 trout weighing 28 lb 9 oz.

In the Hampshire Record Office in Winchester there is a faded notebook. From the entries it seems likely that the unknown diarist was a farmer or landowner at Compton with fishings on the Test which he rented out. He received presents of trout and grayling from Longstock Fishing Club, Stockbridge Club and 'Houghton Club of Gentleman Fishers'. Among the entries are the following:

1823. Fishing. Longstock Fishing Club is this year Sir Chas & Mr Rich, Mr Snow, Rev. Mr Beadon Mr Jerred [This is probably Jarrett, who was received into the Houghton Club on the Longstock Club's termination]. Stockbridge Fishing Club this year.
Rev. Dampier, Sir Charles Bloice [Blois, Bart], Mr Barnard, Mr Chas Taylor, Mr Popham, Mr Beckford 2.
June.
Brook Mr Woodburne's friends began fishing at Brook Mayfly, Lord George Beresford & General Vincent. I fished a little in the even caught one trout about 1 lb, and one do about $2\frac{1}{4}$ lb.

1824.
7 June. I caught 20 fish, Woodburne only 1 or 2, Lascelles 3 or 4, 2 of them 4 lb or more. 15 June. B. Rumbold & R. Judd cut weeds in Lake. My net caught only 1 a good one weighed 4 lb & a little one.

Menu

—

Melon

—

Vraie Tortue en Tasse

—

Filet de Sole Diplomate

—

Médaillon Soufflé Victoria

Velouté Favorite

—

Selle d'Agneau à la Broche

Petits Pois New Jersey

Pommes Persillées

—

Caille en Cocotte New Claridge's

Salade d'Asperges

—

Coeur Flottant Henriette aux Fraises

Mignardises

—

Croûton Bayonnaise

—

Café

Wines.

—

CHÂT.
CARBONNIEUX 1917

—

MOET ET CHANDON
DRY IMPERIAL 1911

—

COCKBURN'S PORT
1904.

—

GRANDS LIQUEURS

—

The menu of the Centenary dinner.

Mr Woodburne was there caught rod and line 2 small ones Lake $1\frac{1}{2}$ lb each. [Lake is a stretch of water at Compton.]

28 May 1830. Houghton Club sent me this morn 1 grayling $1\frac{1}{2}$ lb 1 trout 3 lb, & 1 trout $2\frac{1}{4}$ lb in all $6\frac{3}{4}$ lb.

3 June 1830. This day Mr Woodburne 2 or 3, ... one, Mr Williams one nearly 5 lb. I believe Ld. George & Mr Pearce nothing. I believe Ld. George & Mr Pearce went home this morning. Ld. George took ill with the gout.

5 June. They finished fishing now last day, fly nearly all gone.

6 June. Houghton Club 17 . . . . caught in all 545 lb trout & grayling. Mr Barnard the most and Mr Pen next most – Some of them nearly 4 lb. 20 weighed 65 lb. They caught more large ones this year. . . .

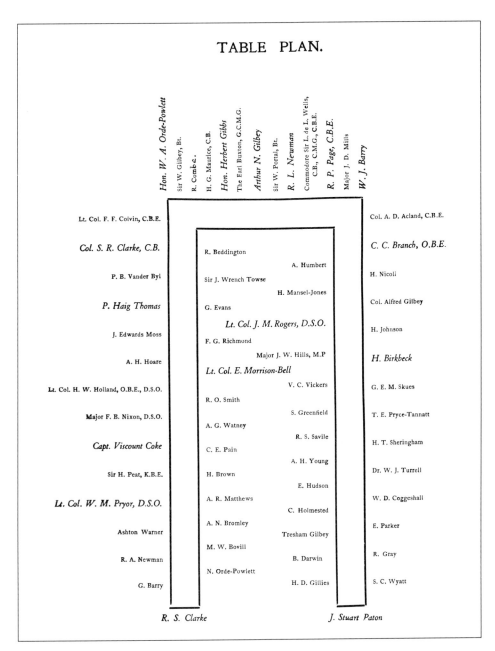

TABLE PLAN.

Hon. W. A. Orde-Powlett
Sir W. Gilbey, Bt.
R. Combe.
H. G. Maurice, C.B.
Hon. Herbert Gibbs
The Earl Buxton, G.C.M.G.
Arthur N. Gilbey
Sir W. Portal, Bt.
R. L. Newman
Commodore Sir L. de L. Wells, C.B., C.M.G., C.B.E.
R. P. Page, C.B.E.
Major J. D. Mills
W. J. Barry

Lt. Col. F. F. Colvin, C.B.E.   Col. A. D. Acland, C.B.E.

Col. S. R. Clarke, C.B. R. Beddington   C. C. Branch, O.B.E.
          A. Humbert

P. B. Vander Byl Sir J. Wrench Towse H. Nicoll
        H. Mansel-Jones

P. Haig Thomas G. Evans   Col. Alfred Gilbey
    Lt. Col. J. M. Rogers, D.S.O.

J. Edwards Moss F. G. Richmond H. Johnson
     Major J. W. Hills, M.P

A. H. Hoare Lt. Col. E. Morrison-Bell H. Birkbeck
      V. C. Vickers

Lt. Col. H. W. Holland, O.B.E., D.S.O. R. O. Smith G. E. M. Skues
      S. Greenfield

Major F. B. Nixon, D.S.O. A. G. Watney T. E. Pryce-Tannatt
      R. S. Savile

Capt. Viscount Coke C. E. Pain H. T. Sheringham
     A. H. Young

Sir H. Peat, K.B.E. H. Brown Dr. W. J. Turrell
     E. Hudson

Lt. Col. W. M. Pryor, D.S.O. A. R. Matthews W. D. Coggeshall
     C. Holmested

Ashton Warner A. N. Bromley E. Parker
    Tresham Gilbey

R. A. Newman M. W. Bovill R. Gray
    B. Darwin

G. Barry N. Orde-Powlett S. C. Wyatt
    H. D. Gillies

R. S. Clarke   J. Stuart Paton

*Table plan for the Centenary dinner. Guests included such celebrated fishermen as
G. E. M. Skues, H. T. Sheringham and J. W. Hills.*

Frederic M. Halford 1844–1914

ONE OF THE BEST REMEMBERED and most influential members of the Houghton Club was Frederic Halford. Intensely interested in insects and their imitation, he was elected a member of the Club in 1877 and thus the Test became his source of natural fly and the water on which to prove his floating patterns. He published the results of his researches in his book *Floating Flies and How to Dress Them* in 1886.

He was not a lone pioneer in this research; George Selwyn Marryat was his partner. Both were skilled anglers, Marryat possibly the superior; both had tenacious probing minds and both stood together at the threshold of the dry fly era. Together they opened the door. Halford acknowledged Marryat's contribution, offering that the book be published in their joint names; we do not know why Marryat declined, but Halford dedicated his second book *Dry Fly fishing in Theory and Practice* (1889) to Marryat.

The thoroughness with which they pursued their inquiries and experiments into the best tackle, lines, flies, dyes, hooks and the tints of natural dubbing furs was typical of the Victorian era. Their aim was: 'To present to the rising fish the best possible imitation of the insect on which he is feeding in its natural position.' Halford expanded this into five necessities:

1. To find a fish feeding on winged insects. (This might be interpreted as an injunction not to fish the water, but seek a single, feeding trout and eschew the sunk fly.)
2. The imitation must resemble the natural in size and colour.
3. The dry fly must float with wings up, i.e. 'cocked'.
4. The fly must alight delicately and drift without drag.
5. Neither rod nor angler must be visible.

It might be imagined that exact imitation required Halford to insist on winged flies. This is not the case. He writes: 'Do not imagine that hackle flies are not good floaters! This is a delusion: when dry they float as well or even better than winged ones, and there is besides one very decided advantage in their use, viz.: that, in whatever position they fall on the water, they are never on their backs or sides, but invariably floating in the natural position.' Many of his dressings are hackled varieties: Detached Badger, Jenny Spinner, Hackle Hare's Ear, Hackle Iron Blue, Coch-y-Bondhu, Hackled Red Ant, amongst many others. In fact he writes of the Detached Badger (his pen name in *The Field*): 'Without wishing to appear egotistical, I consider this the best imitation yet produced of the red spinner.' His dressing was:

HACKLE Badger cock
BODY White horsehair dyed in No. IX, worked over a foundation of doubled bristle also dyed in No. IX, and the body ribbed with crimson tying-silk
HOOK o or oo

E. Crawshaw & Co, London, makers of dyes, produced a set of standard dyes for fly dressers at the suggestion of Halford. No. IX is described as 'red spinner', a pale dried blood colour.

It is not only in the field of fly dressing that our hats should be doffed to Halford. His suggestions on presenting the fly, the care accorded each cast (particularly the first), ring with the truth of experience. His promotion of the horizontal cast with the single-handed rod is based on three factors: concealment by reduced rod silhouette; better cocking and a lighter descent onto the water of winged flies. This second factor, which might be described as a parachute descent, follows power termination in the extended leader parallel to and one foot above the water. The fly then rights itself during descent due to the weight of the hook and 'this cast will "cock" a thoroughly dry fly at least three times out of four.' Additionally 'the angler who can and does use this cast is independent of the direction of the wind.' Today we might describe such a cast as 'cutting under the wind.'

He caters for other matters: the prevention of 'drag'; lifting off well downstream of a trout which has refused; ascertaining accurately the position of each trout. This latter point illustrates detailed thought. He writes that the sound of a rising fish alerts us, we whirl about, see the widening ring or drifting bubble and, by that time 'the ring or bubble made by the fish has been carried some feet down by the current.'

We are fortunate that Halford's contributions to angling literature were made soon after the introduction of single-handed six-section split cane rods; oiled silk tapered fly lines with which one could cast into the wind, and the up-eyed dry fly hook which replaced the eyeless hook whipped to gut.

Thus Halford and the new equipment arrived together. In his writings he celebrated the virtues of the new inventions and expounded the theory of the upstream dry fly. His principles and suggestions are as applicable today as they were one hundred years ago.

A famous trio of Test fishermen: William Senior, Martin E. Mosely, Frederic M. Halford, c 1910.

The HFC Today

MICK LUNN
21 MARCH 1989, IN THE CLUB ROOM
THE DRY FLY

'THE IDEAL SET-UP is a rising fish and tempting him with the size of fly he's taking. The accuracy of the chuck; the wind catered for; to see him come up and take it – that's the tops.' So said Mick, puffing on a cheroot in the bow window, his back to the Stockbridge scene. He continued: 'If I had six fishers who went out and they came back with six fish each at the end of the day, it would be found that they would have been taken on different flies: Caperer, Tups, Iron Blue. What you would then notice is that the majority would have fallen to flies of the same size. Size is more important than pattern or colour. This, coupled to presentation are the crucial factors – more than a purist's correct insect identification.'

Today, with polaroid spectacles, you can spot trout before they see you. In times past one would have trodden on them. The result is the ability to classify trout into those which are feeding near the surface on the hatch, and others which are deep, dormant or nymphing. It is Mick's contention that 'If he's feeding steadily at evening rise on Sherry Spinner, then Sherry Spinner is what you'll catch him on.' Alternatively, if he's deep a large fly may surprise him, raise him and achieve his downfall, 'It is the surprise arrival of a substantial mouthful which does the trick. Let him see the fly fall, not float over him from a long way ahead. Not necessarily right over him, a bit to one side or behind. There seems to be a spot which attracts a trout. Sometimes they turn and follow it down. If it lands behind they don't have time to inspect – a decision has to be taken to grab that fly. My yardstick: feeding fish – small fly; non-feeder – large fly.'

He had found that the trouble with the large fly technique was over-use. 'They come to me and say "He hasn't come up for a bit. I suppose he's gone." I have to reply "Not surprising when you've been bashing him for ages." You can go on and on with a small fly at a fish, but not with a large fly.'

On fishing at night he finds that conditions are rarely favourable, coming right about once in two or three years. 'What is needed is the hatching of a needle sedge in late August or September. There must be a full moon in a cloudless sky. I took a rod out after dinner one night. He caught 13 trout, but when we counted them at the hotel there were only 12 in the bag. He went back to the river and returned with the missing trout.'

Night fishing was advocated by Walton:

Pisc: 'You are to know, there is night as well as day-fishing for a trout; and that, in the night, the best trouts come out of their holes. And the manner of taking them is: on the top of the water, with a great lob or garden-worm, or rather two, ...

And if the night be not dark, then fish so with an artificial fly of a light-colour, and at the snap (that is to say at the first touch of the fish), nay he will sometimes rise at a dead mouse, or a piece of cloth, or anything that seems to swim across the water, or be in motion. This is a choice way. . . .

And you are to know, that in Hampshire – which I think exceeds all England, for swift, shallow, clear, pleasant brooks and store of trouts – they use to catch trouts in the night by the light of a torch or straw; which when they have discovered, they strike with a trout spear, or other ways.'

THE NYMPH

'Nymph fishing is not necessary until the back-end. You can do it all with a dry fly. That's what the game is all about – dry fly fishing. A good upstream nymph man can take fish throughout the season without using a floating fly at all, but that's not the way of things. It is more rewarding to use a fly, see the rise, a fish lift to take – that sort of thing.'

But Mick Lunn considers the system is open to abuse, 'They may start upstream, then it is a bit square and then, before you know where you are, the nymph is trickling about below. That is not playing the game. Neither is the dragging mayfly. Upstream nymph is a fine art, make no mistake. Any fool can throw a nymph at a fish, but it takes a good man to tighten when the fish has eaten it.' He continued: 'Upstream nymph depends on seeing your fish and acting on his movements. Watch his reaction to your nymph, see him stroll across, open his mouth and turn away – that's the time to raise the rod. Or, if you're good enough, look out for the twitch of the cast.' Although skill is involved, Mick feels that it may become a habit with the result that the angler misses the pleasure of the surface rise. 'If you wage war on a fish which is being pernickety, and he doesn't take your Caperer but he looks at it, and at the next dry fly then, by fiddling, you may get him. Try something smaller or something outrageous. It's all fun, and then he takes.

We moved on to nymph patterns: 'Basically you want a nymph to sink; for this a bit of old-fashioned spit is a help. My grandfather invented a Greenwell nymph and an Orange & Partridge. That one had a hot orange body and a bit of a duck wing for a hood. It was sparsely hackled and there was a twist of gold wire up the body. The Greenwell had a black wing case and a yellow body. On No. 16, 14 or 12 hooks they are absolute mustard. I've stuck to them since grandfather's day; they've stood the test of 100 years of use.'

THE CLUB'S FISHING DIARY

Mick weighs trout as they are brought into the hotel, recording the name of the rod and where the fish was taken. The following morning details are entered after breakfast in the Club diary by the senior member present, or by Mick. 'I like to record interesting things about the day. In the old days the entries were more descriptive – who won the Derby and by how many lengths. There was more time in the last century. The coming of the railway enabled rods to come for one day and then return to London. In grandfather's day members came for the mayfly. They would stay for a week or even two and he might not see them again that season.'

TROUT TACKLE

Fine nylon is not encouraged. 'People like to boast of 6X leaders. That is not clever. At Houghton you would lose many trout. At mayfly time use 2X or even 1X. If you are fishing with a No. 8 hook the fly will crack-off on 4X. As the season progresses the water becomes clearer and nylon must be finer.'

He is certain that fish see nylon, particularly in the thin clear water of September. 'At that time you've got one or two experienced Georges and Freds about who've seen it all before. The resident fishermen, who know all about Fred and George, do not waste time on them. They take a couple of throws, not very well done, and set off up the river. A newcomer, fishing fine and with care, plots and achieves their downfall.'

THE LUNN DYNASTY

William James Lunn was born in London on 2 January 1862. After a hard and varied early life he came to the Test at the age of 24. On 1 January 1887 he succeeded James Faithfull as keeper of the Houghton water, and took up residence in a cottage at Sheepbridge Shallow. William's son, Alfred, served in the Royal Flying Corps during the Great War, was demobilized in 1919, came to the Test and served his apprenticeship under his father. William retired in 1931 and was succeeded by Alfred as head-keeper at the time when motor cars were coming into general use. Most of William's keepering had been on the lower Houghton water. If he wished to visit Goddard, the keeper of the Stockbridge area, he had to walk up to the town. A car made all the difference to mobility in Alfred's time; he was able to oversee the whole water. In 1936 the family moved to Stock-bridge, to Test Lea, which is Mick's present home. Alfred was head-keeper for 31 years and was succeeded by Mick, who had served under his father since leaving school.

REARING AND STOCKING TROUT

Stocking has changed little in numbers, but the average size has crept up, due to better rearing conditions and food. Until 25 years ago fish were fed minced horseflesh, cockles and mussels, and cod flaps. The mincing and mixing of these was unpleasant, particularly in hot weather. The development of the trout pellet, preferably made from fish rather than other animal protein, improved growth rates and the handling of the feed. Today a trout may be grown in one year to a size that would have taken two years on the old diet.

When Mick became head-keeper the size of trout stocked averaged $1\frac{1}{2}$ lb. Today fish are introduced at between 2 lb and $2\frac{1}{2}$ lb. In his early days a two pounder was a good fish. And everyone came to look at a three-pounder! 'Nowadays a 3 lb fish is quite common. You only go and look at 7 or 8 pounders.'

He does not consider it sensible on a river to compete with other fisheries on size of trout. 'On still waters, one man takes a 10 lb fish and the next water has to provide an 11 lb trout to remain in the picture.' On the Houghton water there is a good spread of sizes, based on the 2 lb fish. Stocking takes place twice a year. Their fishing is extensive, there being 15 miles of fishable bank. On such a length, and because on some days only two or three rods are fishing, the trout become truly wild. It follows that they are also uneducated, free rising and hence more catchable than those on some syndicated fisheries where 'Every time a trout rises something is whanged over his head.' The stocking ratio is $\frac{2}{3}$ brown trout to $\frac{1}{3}$ rainbows, with the latter introduced in the second half of the season.

Over the years inflation has made it necessary to sell trout; members' subscriptions are no longer sufficient to service the fishery. In 1960 Alfred Lunn was asked to produce for the outside market. There had always been a small excess of trout over requirements and this slight over-production was enlarged. Today 20 to 25,000 catchable trout are produced and much of the Test is stocked from Houghton. This work is labour intensive. 'There are three beats: middle, upper and lower. There is a keeper on each. A man works in the hatchery, and there is a general factotum who travels between the beats helping with weed cutting, mudding, mowing and so on. I do a bit of everything.'

THE WORKING YEAR

'When the rods go after the final day of September my season starts.' The first task is to clear the river of coarse fish. Grayling and pike are removed by netting and electric fishing.

Spawning then begins on the fish farm. The breeding stock has been selected throughout the year on shape, colour and size on the principle that like breeds like. The spawning activity sets off the hatchery. Then there is the river activity: preparing for the following season. Between November and January banks are trimmed and repaired, mud is moved and stiles and bridges repaired. Stocking takes place in April. During the fishing season weeds are cut during those periods set aside by the Test and Itchen Fishing Association. In between weed cuts, banks are mown and fringes topped.

Our morning coffee had grown cold on the club-room table; I had taken notes and recorded our conversations; photographs had been taken; two hours had passed. 'Let's have some lunch downstairs in the bar. Why don't you come back in May? Take some photographs of the river.' I did!

Mick Lunn in The Houghton Club room. Mick, his father Alfred and grandfather William have held the position of head keeper to the Club since 1887.

Fairey Estate, Bossington

BRIAN PARKER — TROUT-KEEPER
20 JUNE AND 6 JULY 1989

Brian came to bossington as head-keeper in March 1986 after 12 years as under-keeper at Broadlands. Above him on the Test are the waters of the Houghton Club and below lies Mottisfont. In between are Brian's four miles of river, divided into eight beats and numbered from one at the downstream end to eight at the top. He is young, fit and resourceful. If the need is to build a fry pond, or remove a fallen tree from the river, he will find a way to carry out the work himself with Gordon, his assistant. Versatility on a river is essential: mudding, mowing and moving on poachers has to be complemented by the ability to dress and fish a No. 18 Iron Blue however rough one's fingers.

I have had the good fortune to be invited to fish the Fairey waters in June. For three seasons, an October day at grayling has come my way, with gourmet lunches laid in the No. 6 hut by Tony and Frances Allen and Brian's wife Lindsay. Memories of autumn days, golden with sun-warmed leaves, last one through the winter.

WEED CUTTING AND MUDDING

There are three cutting periods during the fishing season. The first is the major cut of the year, in 1989 from 13 to 24 June. 'I tend to be violent in my treatment of the weeds in June; then I'm on top of them for the rest of the season.'

The next cut was short. The six days 24 to 29 July are not sufficient to cover the whole river, but allow time to tidy up anything missed in June.

The final cut is a month later: 21 to 31 August. This cutting period is too late and too long in Brian's opinion 'It is not necessary to do much if you have cut thoroughly in June and July, and the whole river will be cleared as soon as the season ends on 30 September.'

Four cutting methods are used: Turk scythe, pole scythe, link scythe and the weed cutting boat. The 11 knives of the link are each about 3 feet long. They are bolted together and at each end of this chain or gang is a shackle to which is tied a rope. With two men on each side of the river the scythe is worked upstream, allowing it to sink at intervals to the bed of the river. This method is used in deep water where it would be too time-consuming or deep for chest waders and a pole scythe. The weed cutting boat is hired by the day for extensive areas of water.

The cutting method depends on what is most suited to a particular stretch of water. Thus, on Beats 1, 2 and 3, which are deep, the links come into use. Beats 4 and 5 are wide. To cut their extensive areas Ron Wilton's cutting boat is brought over from the river Itchen. Beats 6, 7 and 8, being narrow and shallow enough for wading, are cut by hand.

Brian leaves bars of weed protruding from the deeper side of the river. These bars slow up the flow of the river, holding it back, and are particularly desirable on the deep side if that bank is not used by the rods. He then cuts drastically on the favoured side. This speeds up the flow of shallow water, scours the bed and channels the river into half of its width. Sometimes the links are used to 'top off' weed beds by skimming downstream close to the surface. Rafts of drifting weed then pass unhindered, are not held up and then lifted off by a rise in the river to drift away outside the weed cutting period.

I watched Brian at work with a pole scythe on Beat 3. He cut mare's tail, wild watercress and carrot weed which has a thick stem resembling cow parsley. Ranunculus is encouraged. In the weed were tiny fish, trout fry and minnows 'You stir up a lot of goodies which brings them on the feed.' Nymphs and caddis are disturbed, but drop off the drifting vegetation to find another home. The final cut takes place after the end of the season on 30 September. The whole river is cleared, opening the bed for mud removal.

Mud is washed downstream by raking the bed, by fixing corrugated iron sheets strategically to increase flows, or by a movable wooden boom. This last device is held across the river by ropes and moved downstream a few yards at a time. Below the boom are boards reaching almost to the river bed; compression speeds the water flow through this narrow gap, dislodging silt which swirls away.

These practices all result in the mud arriving in the waters of your down-

TOP *Brian Parker cutting the weed with a pole scythe at Bossington.*
BELOW *A set of heavy link scythes.*

stream neighbour. There is more silt than in earlier years. Roger Tym, who rents a section of the top Bossington water, puts this down to intensive cultivation right up to the river bank, from which the ploughed field is separated by a single ditch. At one time fields now planted with wheat or maize were permanent water meadows. These were 'drowned' in winter, providing an early bite of frost-protected grass for cattle, and acting as a water filter and silt settling area. Today's storms flush soil from cultivated fields into open ditches through which the silt is carried to the river. Roger has done much work in fencing cattle from the banks of his section, helped by Brian Parsons, a contractor who improved the river bed by working downstream with a tracked digger. He built up the banks with the mud and stones dug out of the bed, and the banks were then seeded with grass.

REARING AND STOCKING

There are two categories of takable trout in the Bossington waters: those, both brown and rainbow, stocked directly at an average weight of 2 lb into the 8 beats; browns reared from ova on the estate by Brian. His intention is to reduce the number of purchased trout, and he is succeeding. The season before his arrival saw the purchase of 2400 trout for direct stocking; this influx has been reduced to 1900, but the total catch has increased. Wild, or semi-wild, browns are more than filling the gap. This is his programme. Let us witness events in the trout rearing year, beginning in the autumn of 1988.

In October Brian helped Guy Robinson at Leckford. They stripped browns, mixing the eggs and milt in a bowl, stirring the contents with a feather. In the middle of that month Brian brought his share to Bossington where they hatched on Christmas Eve. For three or four weeks the hatched alevins are nourished by the yolk sac suspended beneath their tiny bellies. When the sac has been absorbed they are supplied with different grades of trout food, starting at Double o and increasing to No. 6, according to their size. The food is made available through an automatic clockwork feeder, although problems arise in deterring hungry mice! By July the fry vary in size: some have achieved 6 in but others have not done so well. On 6 July I attended the grading of his 4000 fry into two categories: large and small. It is as simple as that. The large ones will be fed on and the little fellows, after an interval, will find their way into the river.

TOP *Cutting weed with a Turk scythe.*
BELOW *Staked sheets of corrugated iron make a sluice to shift mud.*

It was a hot morning. I asked whether it would be sensible to grade
the troutlets as the water would, surely, be warm. Brian responded that
the water in the fry pond would not exceed 55°F. Nearby, in a thick wood,
Brian had found a spring from which water welled at a temperature of 51°F.
He channelled this through the pond he built to house the fry. On arrival
we took the temperature of the flow after it had passed through the pond.
The thermometer read 52°F. We then tested the river, finding this to be
66°F. The water, having passed through the pond, flows into a ditch 700
yards in length, and from there disgorges into the river. In hot weather
trout swim from the river into the ditch, seeking oxygen, shade and cool
water.

The fry had been starved for 48 hours and were now moved half way

On dark nights eels run down-river.

down the fry pond which is 40 yards in length, 1 yard wide and 1 foot
deep. Compressed into a short section before a screen they were netted and
passed through the bars of a Grice & Young grader borrowed from Kimbridge. Those which fell through the grader, the small fish, dropped into
the downstream end of the stew from which they would make their way,
in a month or two, into the river. Large fry were returned to the top pond.
The favoured 2000 are fed until the end of the season when, at lengths
varying between 6 and 8 inches, they are introduced into the river. By the
time these brownies reach a takable size they will be wild. In April 1989
Tony Allen and I caught two trout of 1 lb 2 oz; Brian thought they would
have been released in the river in the autumn of 1987 as 4 oz fry.

Bought fish will be stocked directly into the river six times during the

Gutted and salted eels ready for smoking.

season. I witnessed the first stocking, by Guy Robinson, of trout from Leck-ford on 26 April. 150 brown and 100 rainbows were introduced, spread throughout the beats. The next stocking, prior to the mayfly, was of rainbows and a third, a 'top-up' followed at the end of May. Brian likes rainbows to go in when there is plenty of food – they rise well to the mayfly. After the mayfly food becomes less plentiful and 'Rainbows will grub about on the bottom.' At this stage he switches to brown trout which rise better when food is sparse. 'When the grub [mayfly] is there the rainbow will be "first up".'

Following the mayfly comes the June weed out during which period both trout and fishermen are in the way. With the cut completed two more stockings take place before the July cut, then one in August and two more before the end of the season.

INSECTS

In January and February, the time of the grayling man, a few iron blues and olives hatch. Fly activity is thin in early spring. Hawthorn arrive at the end of April, plentiful in recent seasons. Between the hawthorn and the mayfly 'An iron blue may pop-up on a cold day.'

In 1989 there was a short, but heavy, hatch of mayfly. It started early in the month, was set back by a short cold spell and then, by 12 May they were drifting by in clouds. On three nights swarms of spent fell back on the river, promising a splendid season in 1991. The sedge is about by June, often in the morning, and the Caperer takes a toll. In July there is the blue-winged olive which, along with the sedge, supports the angler until the end of the season. The brave iron blue, a tiny but tough insect, sails down the valley on metallic wings on cold days of his choosing.

BOSSINGTON GRAYLING AND A RAINBOW TROUT

It has become fashionable to fish solely the fly for grayling, trout and salmon, but who has not, as a child, impaled two maggots on a hook, watched a red-topped float, and struck when it went under? I was reminded of those days when fishing the Test in October.

The brown trout season had closed. Brian showed me where to fish for grayling, and said I might also take a rainbow trout on fly, for they have no close season and lose condition through the winter. Forty years had passed since last I watched a cork or quill, but the fascination was recaptured. Hooking grayling in this manner is not simple; you have to time it right. First there is the tremble, then the bob, then the sliding away and the submersion. All stages must be endured before the rod is raised.

'The Lady of the Stream' she is called, and rightly so. Slim in shape, translucent in the fin and delicate in flavour. She also takes a fly, rising more steeply than trout, shooting up lightly before returning to the river bed. Trout patrol near the surface, on the fin, rolling over the fly, luxuriously sucking it down. Both fish were rising steadily by mid-morning. Discarding the trotting rod loaned to me by Tony I converted to the fly, setting up an 8 foot split cane. There is something about cane which blends with a chalk stream – perhaps the leisurely action matches the progress of the river. Chalk streams have been with us for centuries, since England was born. Cane also has a pedigree.

On that warm day which fly should be tied to the point of my 5 X leader? I did not ponder long, seated on a bench at the waterside, a fly box on my knees. If blue-winged olives are in the air and a few late-hatching sedge drift up the valley on a southern breeze, I go for a Wickham's Fancy. Trout and grayling like a Wickham. Perhaps it is the glint of gold tinsel on the body and the warmth of the red cock hackle. Few fish reject that fly, but if they do I try a midge, a hackled black one, and put my trust in that.

Enchanting as the scene may be, a seated fisherman, if he is worthy of the name, remains alert. The black nose breaking the surface to suck down a fly, the sliding dorsal fin and waving tail which stretch the water skin – must be noticed; catch his eye. My rainbow, which he became, because I ate him, rose mid-river without revealing his aldermanic size. His rise was a sip, a tiny whorl. Into this vortex went a fly, permanently. Others followed. So steady a feeder invited rash action. Instead I studied his position, took note of protecting weeds, worked out currents which might cause the fly to drag across his window to put him down. A deception was plotted. With this done, and humbly out of sight upon my knees I approached to make my throw, I took a look behind – there stood a willow festooned with angler's flies. Out went the line, the leader uncurled across the weed, the fly alighted upright on fine hackles and he took! He plunged, thrashed his tail. All to no avail. The net slid beneath his portly shape and down he went to Devon in my car.

TONY ALLEN'S BOSSINGTON SALMON

The fish revealed himself by following a hooked trout to the net. He was vast. He lay two rod lengths off, swaying in the current. Tony lacked a fly.

Brian arrived, followed by another rod in a Land Rover. He had a fly on the ledge below the windscreen, a double, missing one hook. The tattiness of the fly a virtue by reason of past popularity with salmon.

The fly was tied to a cut-down 4X leader and cast by a short trout rod. The salmon was indifferent at first. Then it took notice. On the third throw the fly was gripped between white-rimmed jaws. The first half of him was shaken into the trout net and the rest drooped out behind. He weighed $8\frac{1}{2}$ lb. It was the final day of the season.

Compton Estate

CECIL HILL — TROUT-KEEPER
19 JANUARY 1989

On the morning of 19 January 1989 I met James Hancock and Mick Lunn in the Houghton Club. James and I then drove south from Stockbridge, through King's Somborne, and passed the entrance to Compton Manor estate office. Compton was the home of Sir Thomas Sopwith. He had celebrated his 101st birthday the day before. The long span of his adventurous life came to an end later in the spring. Childhood memories of constructing balsa wood models of that Great War fighter plane the Sopwith Camel floated across my mind. Passing the entrance we turned right to cross the dismantled Stockbridge/Romsey railway line on which I had travelled as a passenger in the 1950s. Recollections surfaced of steam engines puffing, iron wheels clanking on iron lines, regular but fleeting views from carriage windows of the winding river and the wildlife of the valley. We drove across a bridge over the disused track and there, spread before us, were flat water meadows and beyond, as Bernard Aldrich described that clear jewel 'the ever rolling stream'. Not only was the river rolling along in good heart, but wildlife also flourished. Small brown pimples of molehills freckled the green meadows. A flock of fieldfares skimmed the grass in looping flight 'chack-chacking' as they went.

All we could see of Cecil as we bumped closer to the fishing hut were his head and shoulders protruding above the bank of a carrier. Cecil was 'mudding'. Clouds of grey silt, shifted by his rake, drifted away downstream as, thigh-booted, he emerged. Shake hands with Cecil and that craggy face, weathered by wind, water and the summer sun, is evidence that here is a man, approaching retirement, who has given his life to the Test. Cecil's grandfather and father were river-keepers on the Kennet, having come from Norfolk in 1913. His father then went to Wherwell to work for Lady Brecknock's father, Col. Jenkins. There, Hill senior built the Wherwell estate trout hatchery in 1930.

The three of us stood and talked by the wooden fishing hut which had been given a coat of green paint over white. The hut is more elaborate than one would expect of a shelter for rods, weighing fish, a plan of the water under the veranda, and angler's resting place. 'That's the old pavilion from the estate cricket ground. We dismantled and brought it here.' It was a morning of clear air, bright sky, sparkling river, and snowdrops by the hut. The waters at the fishing hut are carriers. These are fished by Compton. The main river across the valley is fished by Bossington rods. Above the bridge on which we stood is The Lake, an open expanse of water leading to The Straight Cut – a trouty place. There are eight beats on Cecil's water, for the eight rods in the syndicate. James was the original member and has fished this water for 15 years.

The season commences on 1st April. James and Cecil gave me an analysis of the fishing months. In 1988 there was a shortage of fly but this may improve now that the farm has ceased to spray the meadows. They expect early spring olives after lunch in April, also iron blues, plenty of those, but only a few grannom. Mayfly start to hatch in mid-May and tail off after the first few days of June when the blue-winged olive takes over. There are plenty of sedges from June onwards and, unlike those of my home waters in the West Country, the Compton sedges hatch early, after breakfast. The fishing is good until mid-June; July is bad; August better; September better still.

Close to the hut is the trout hatchery, the stews, and the old pump house with brass pump and ancient wooden paddle wheel now still and lifeless after close on a hundred years. There was an older pump which was replaced in 1959. Neither pump nor wheel work today. The system was installed to move water through the hatchery and stews, but these are now disused due to poaching. Today Compton buy in their trout from Houghton who stock directly into the river. Compton have 1200 browns and rainbows ordered for the 1989 season and these will go in at a weight of about 2 lb. Below the pump house is the eel trap. This is operated by closing down the sluices on the main carrier and opening those which discharge into a square enclosure with an iron grid base. Eels enter on their downstream migration back to the Sargasso Sea, are stranded on the grid and raked into a holding receptacle. Eels travel at night, from June onwards, between full moons when all is black as pitch. The keeper has to be up throughout the hours of darkness to keep the grid raked clear of drifting weed. Originally, after the war, there were ten wooden hatches across The Lake: five for the carrier and five for the eel rack. The eels are taken up to Mick Lunn's at Houghton where all the keepers congregate. A dealer comes down from London with a lorry and oxygenated tanks.

James, being President of the British Trust for Ornithology, presented me with an opportunity to learn more of the bird life of the valley. That morning, before we arrived, Cecil saw a great black-backed gull take a $2\frac{1}{2}$ lb brown trout in the shallows by the hut. The weight was not a guess – he weighed the fish from which the bird had picked the eyes and gills. A flock of lapwings had been on the meadows and golden plover frequented the downs above Chilbolton. Cecil knows of a wood which is home to a pair of long-eared owls.

We saw ducks on the water: mallard, teal, tufted, wigeon, pochard. Some had paired and one or two were nesting, the winter being abnormally mild. A ruddy duck put in an appearance. James told me there were kestrels, sparrowhawks and an occasional hobby. Kingfishers would return to nest in the spring, warblers as well before the buds burst and the leaves on the trees unfurled. James has a liking for grey wagtails even though they are inaptly named, being mostly yellow. There were four pairs in 1988, one of which brought off three broods just below the hatches. Wagtails enjoy rich feeding by the river and are as keen on flies as trout. Of the rarer birds there are water rails, and a pair of barn owls nested in an old tree. The tree blew down in a storm and two owl boxes have been installed in a copse as replacement homes.

Sedge and reed warblers, buntings too, chitter in the rushes by day, and tawny and little owls shiver the mice at night with eerie cries. Blackcaps put in an appearance as does the lesser spotted woodpecker. August brings a southward migration of greenshank and curlew, an occasional redshank and, once or twice, an osprey drifts down the valley.

I asked Cecil the hours when he recommended his members to fish. 'The Houghton Club members often fish at night and sometimes don't get back to the hotel before midnight. They have dinner at 8.30 pm and then go out.' 'With faltering step', interjected James. 'But old Sir Thomas wouldn't have that', continued Cecil, 'He said "If you haven't caught your fish between 10 am and 6 pm you may not go down again".'

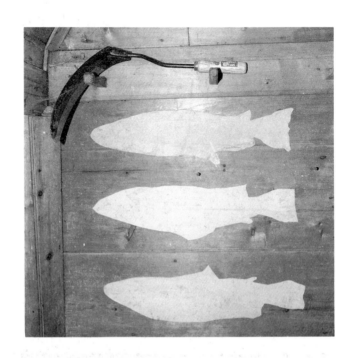

Compton

THE THATCHED HUT

THE FISHING HUT HAS STOOD by the river for over 100 years. It has the appearance of a dark, over-mature, thick-stemmed horse mushroom. Thatch overhangs the black tarred wooden walls and I hit my head on the straw eaves when making for the door. Inside it was dark. Shafts of sunlight knifed through cracks in wooden shutters which protected the glass window panes. I undid four bolts, removed two long iron straps made by a blacksmith and swung open the black wood covers. As the light seeped in I half expected to see a committee of ancient bearded anglers seated on the long benches which flanked the wooden table. The hut was silent, empty of all but memories of former generations and the tackle of those now taking their turn. Particles of dust floated in sunbeams and then re-settled on the table, the benches and the wooden stools.

Across the wooden rack were two rods: an 8 ft 6 in Hardy Palakona, and a tough pike spinning rod. On pegs to the left were five trout nets, open, ready for work. By the door the outlines of monster trout, traced around, then cut from paper, caught on mayfly in years gone by, were stuck on the planks of the wall. A lantern hung from the ceiling and another, with matches, stood on the table. Not all of fishing is catching fish; bottles were on a shelf. There was a gas cooker, candles, a kettle, and pads of paper on which to record the catch.

Pulling a torch from my bag I examined writings on the walls. Sometimes a nail had been used to scratch a record, sometimes a pen. Pencil predominated. Who was the mystery keeper who cleared the river of 135 pike between 1878 and 1882? Whoever he was, the trout benefited.

OPPOSITE TOP *The Thatched Hut, Compton. 'By the door the outlines of monster trout traced around.'*
BELOW *The Thatched Hut, Compton.*

W. R. Cheadle wrote with a shaky hand. How old was he?
1886. June 3. Mayfly. $3\frac{3}{4}$. $3\frac{1}{4}$. 4 lb
1888. June 13. $4\frac{1}{2}$. $4\frac{1}{4}$. $8\frac{3}{4}$ lb
A man of few words, scarce stirred by $8\frac{3}{4}$ lb. We would like to read more
of his ways, but he is reticent, concluding his era with
1889. April 20, 22. $2\frac{3}{4}$. $3\frac{1}{2}$. W.R.C.

G.A.S. is expansive
G.A.S. 1895. April 23. 1 beauty of $2\frac{3}{4}$ lb

Progress into the 20th century.
6 trout. 18 lb 7 oz. 4/6/1900. Lt. G.C.D.

Six years pass. A military man shatters the tranquil scene:
1906. June 2. 1 pike $18\frac{1}{2}$ lb. Shot by Capt. I. Ramsden in Lake.

Perhaps Capt. I. Ramsden had a relative for there are two entries.
1906. May 11. 8 trout 19 lb 8 oz. C. Ramsden
1906. June 3. 5 trout 12 lb 14 oz. C. Ramsden.

Head keeper Cecil Hill of Compton has netted the first trout of the season ($3\frac{1}{2}$lb brown) for doyen rod James Hancock.

A skilful hunter now takes up his pencil. Trout are not for him. He is selective. Large grayling are the quarry. Nothing else will do. He records no trout.

1906. July 14. 1 grayling 3 lb 7 oz. C. A. Campbell

1907. July 22. 1 grayling 3 lb 2 oz. C.A.C.

1907. July 27. 1 grayling 3 lb 3 oz. C.A.C.

Between 1924 and 1926 Alfred Herbert caught many trout and M. H. Pepper a grayling of 3 lb 4 oz. Other rods who recorded their catch were: Florence Herbert, J. W. Downing, H. Bankes Price, F. M. Haig, M. H. Peppiat, Neville Smith, R. M. Bushby and Michael Forbes.

The war is fought. Alfred Herbert is defiant.

1941. May 12. 1 trout $2\frac{1}{2}$ lb.

A. H. HITLER BE DAMNED

The Second World War, being over in Europe, there is time to fish.

1945. April 30. 1 trout 2 lb 15 oz. 1 grayling 12 oz. Lt. Mason. R.N.R.

The state of the river and of the country after the war disturbs Herbert who is still going strong and does not mince his words.

1948. July 14. One trout $1\frac{3}{4}$ lb. In spite of the Catchment Board and the Labour Government. A.H.

Someone else scribbles:

19.8.49. Hut tarred and thatched in spite of the Labour Government. E.I.L.

Years pass. Anglers fish. Trout die. Lovers stroll the banks and a good man takes the plunge beside the flowing water:

1959. May 17.

JOHN. B. RAY and JUDITH CLARKE

affianced here this day. Not fish but 4 bottles of Champers taken from the river.

Attention seems to be straying from the river to those sheltered by the hut:

1962. Aug 3. Belinda Ray. 8 lb 4 oz when caught. Now 16 lb at 4 months.

Youth or whiskery old age? Boy or dog? Wonder with me on this:
1965. June 2. C. Philip Porritt caught his first trout. Whiskers Porritt caught
his first mole.

The most recent entry fills me with speculation. Was she blond or brunette?
I feel she was slim and graced the scene. Sandra Elvers-Dix. The name flows
off the tongue. Slim green wellies for Sandra. A silk scarf about her locks.
Miss Sandra Elvers-Dix. 1st brown trout from the Test. 2 lb o oz. 29/5/1979.

In the late afternoon of that June day I went fishing after recording these
bygone events. Bill Heller, who has the fishing, invited me and I made up
my tackle in the hut. I am indebted to Bill who did not hesitate over the
telephone in granting permission to view the writings on the wall 'and bring
a rod with you'. In the back of the car, brought up from Devon, is my
Smuggler. Eight pieces of carbon fibre were fitted together. Marquis No.
7 reel mounted, and a floating line run through the rings. I knotted on
a 5X tapered leader and wandered down the river. A chill north wind blew
straight downstream. Not a fly hatched, but a few smuts and midges danced
under the trees. The river was dead, or so it seemed to the casual sweeping
glance. The trout must have been glutted by the mayfly of the previous
month. A weed cut was in progress. A hot cloudless June day. Not promising. Down I went. Hot footstep after hot footstep I followed those aristocratic banks. This was the Test. I could not fail. To write about the river
and then admit a blank would be unthinkable.

Then there was a dimple, a tiny pimple of a rise, tucked under the bank,
my bank, below a thistle. There are thistles on the Test. A trout. I could
see him taking smuts. On the third cast the No. 18 Black Gnat caught on
the thistle and the trout went down. Fifty yards below a second trout rose.
He suffered my attentions bravely but departed on the sixth blown-back
cast. Around the corner the wind blew from right to left. Almost a helpful

OPPOSITE TOP *Bridge joining Hermit Lodge (right) where the Prince of Wales
(later Edward VII) used to stay for Stockbridge races, and the White House,
temporary residence for the race meeting of Lillie Langtry. An earlier wooden bridge
collapsed under the prince at night, depositing him in the river.*
BELOW *Leckford Estate. Brown trout being measured for stocking.*

wind. To the rear a dead blackthorn stood its ground. Far out, on a flat water, in oily stillness, a fish pushed up the water skin. Nothing opulent. Not breathtaking. A rise the size of a grain of rice. The insect was tiny. My smallest flies are No. 18 Iron Blues and Black Gnats. The latter was tied on with all the delicacy of Major Turle and then dunked and shaken in the floatant bottle. Out flew the line, the leader extended, the fly drifted perfectly over the trout. Nothing happened. Again the line covered the width between me and the trout but a puff of wind caught this perfect cast. The leader fell in concentric circles with the fly in the middle like a bull's eye. The trout took. This 2 lb brownie had a liking for weed. Growing, or floating drifting weed, it didn't matter. He just went for weed. In he went. I pulled him out. His mother must have told him weed was a good thing. The 5X nylon held. He is now in Devon in my freezer, but I dared not write on the wooden wall.

OPPOSITE TOP *View of the Test towards Leckford from The Grange, Longstock, clubhouse of the old Longstock Fishing Club.*
BELOW *The Fishing Cottage, Upper Clatford, on the river Anton.*

119

Lower Brook House. Control room at Alan Mann's salmon hatchery.

Lower Brook House, King's Somborne

ALAN MANN — SALMON HATCHERY OWNER
3 MAY 1989

Aʟᴀɴ's sᴀʟᴍᴏɴ ꜰᴀʀᴍɪɴɢ ᴇɴᴛᴇʀᴘʀɪsᴇ is based in Scotland where he has several hatcheries. Why then did he, three years ago, decide to hatch salmon ova on the Test, with all the additional capital expenditure involved? As he explained, it is to take advantage of a natural phenomenon. In Scotland, at the season when ova are maturing to hatch, the water temperature is 3° or 4° Centigrade. At the same time of year water may be pumped out of the chalk aquifer alongside the Test at 10°C. In Scotland 90 days are needed to hatch an egg, but only 28 days are necessary in the Test valley. That is one advantage. Others follow. In Scotland he is able to produce from ova 80% smolts in 16 months. Known as S1 smolts they have matured through the stages ova, alevin, fry and parr in that period. In the spring parr become silver in colour, a transition termed 'to smoltify', and are ready to swim down river to the sea. All well and good, but once in every four or five years in Scotland they have a cold spring or autumn and the production of S1 smolts drops to 50% or less. As a result, to stabilize production, he looked at the possibility of incubating eggs and first feeding the alevins in the south.

Starting 10 years ago he sent eggs down to trout farms, but the results were not good. It was difficult to persuade the trout men that salmon were a separate species, requiring different treatment. Three years ago he installed equipment to raise young salmon on the Test. Courage was required; the history of raising salmon on the river did not give rise to confidence. He has now been hatching and first feeding at Lower Brook House for three seasons with few problems. These are his methods:

Freshly fertilized eggs are called 'green'. Salmon ova are very sensitive until they are 'eyed' at about 250 degree days (days × °C). Once the egg is 'eyed' it becomes more durable and, as Alan says, 'May be bounced upon the floor.' Such ova may be sent around the world by air. Present research is showing that eggs are at their most sensitive between six and 10 days after fertilization, when shock will kill them. But, they may, in safety, be moved immediately after fertilization, and that is what he does. If fish are stripped and the ova fertilized at 11 am in Ullapool, packed on ice and flown south, they arrive none the worse on the Test the same evening.

Because ova hatch quickly on the Test, first feeding can begin at the end of January, when the alevins weigh 0.15 to 0.16 grams. In $3\frac{1}{2}$ weeks they double their weight, and as we spoke on 3 May the hatchery had alevins weighing 0.8 to 0.9 grams. In Scotland their counterparts had just started first feeding. The Test fish will be 100 to 150 gram smolts next spring, at which time their Scottish brethren will weigh 50 to 60 grams. During this third year of operation Alan expects to send $3\frac{1}{4}$ million alevins back to Scotland by air.

We left the house and crossed the river to visit the hatchery where there are 22 tanks of $1\frac{1}{2}$ metres diameter equipped with self feeders. In some inserts are used to reduce the depth to about 1 foot for the first feeding stage. This first phase is tricky, because the alevins are difficult to distribute evenly in the tank. With an insert reducing the depth, it is easier to control feeding and water flows for the first month or six weeks. When the alevins are feeding well the insert is removed and they can utilize the full depth. Each tank is capable of holding 25,000 to 35,000 small fish.

All water is pumped up from boreholes, then passed under an ultra-violet filter to remove any possible contamination. After circulating through the tanks it is pumped back into the aquifer. No water is thus lost; no excreta goes into the river, and the volume of excreta is, in any case, tiny in comparison with a trout farm. The only disadvantage of the system is the reliance on mechanical and electrical pumping which could be subject to breakdown. In Scotland the water flow is by gravity. In addition to the indoor first feeding tanks there are three 3-metre tanks, away from the buildings, close to the river. These accommodate large parr while they grow to smolt stage.

What has the hatchery to do with Test salmon fishing? At first glance the investment might appear to be a Scottish enterprise taking advantage of the warmth of the south solely for commercial reasons and returning nothing to the valley. This is not so. Alan, an energetic, successful man, has amalgamated the needs of his business with the needs of the Test. He breeds salmon for the river and I doubt not, though he made no mention, that he subsidizes the process so far as the Test is concerned. He does it because it interests him. 'When I started I had a great deal of help from local people because I was not just another trout farm. Salmon are having a bad time on the Test. I took the view that the salmon farmers and riparian owners had a lot to offer each other. I have had help from Mick Lunn, Test & Itchen, John Potter and Southern Water.'

We sat on in his kitchen where a diagram of the salmon life cycle hangs on the wall and the window looks out on to the river valley. 'The programme on the Test is to try to re-establish a viable volume of fish spawning naturally in the river. Re-stocking could not be afforded as a continuous process because smolts are expensive. We want to give the river a short-term boost in the hope that it will become permanent. Whether the physical condition of the river is now suitable is a matter which only time will reveal.'

Alan went on: 'One of the problems facing the local salmon rehabilitation effort was catching-up sufficient adult stock for stripping. Last year, after Christmas, Southern Water only obtained 50,000 eggs. Three years ago I took 30,000 eggs off them and quarantined them in an outdoor trough in Scotland in case they had any disease. In the meantime Southern Water sent the parent stripped fish off to their Weymouth branch to see if they had any infections.' Those 30,000 eggs have proved fruitful and their product will multiply. Alan has two-year classes of Test fish in Scotland. The first batch has been in the sea since the spring of 1988, and he should obtain grilse eggs from them this autumn. He would like to have 5000 Test fish from those grilse, then any amount of eggs could be made available from brood fish. By this discerning and lengthy process Test salmon can come back to the Test.

In February 1989 they had 20,000 smolts at Lower Brook House: 5000 in each of two 3-metre tanks and 10,000 in the third. To reduce the density of fish in the 10,000 tank Alan put 5000 out at Broadlands in February. The remaining 15,000 were due to be released at the end of April, but one morning there were mortalities in one of the tanks. Taking a risk they released all the smolts early at Testwood, Nursling and Broadlands. It is a fine judgement to decide when to release smolts. If put out too early they will delay in the river and lose condition; if too late they may not be fully imprinted by the river and then fail to return to that river after their sea life.

It has been said by salmon farming critics that smolts from a hatchery may not be as fit as natural smolts. Alan comments: 'If hatchery smolts can swim all the way to Greenland and back there cannot be much wrong with them. If you put a trout in the river it stays there all the time. If a salmon smolt is sent to sea it has to go through the vast oceanic filter.' It seemed clear to me that such a fish would breed healthy capable offspring.

I drove away to 'The Plough' at King's Somborne, pondering the while on all I had seen and heard. I had met a man who had no axe to grind. He did not own or rent a salmon fishery on the Test. Pioneering is expensive, full of risk. He was *giving* a service to the river in return for a simple benefit: warm spring water.

Oakley Stream

JOHN WALLER HILLS

'T HE FISHING OF OUR YOUTH was the fishing of a past age, and we are able to describe a state of things which no longer exists.'

In those words Hills justified for authors in general and himself in particular the writing of angling books. In *A Summer on the Test* he described fishing days in the early years of the 20th century. His record, that pause in the unfolding years as seasons passed and all grow older, was his excuse for yet another book. Yet another? One doubts that another exists in which the water buttercups sway more luxuriantly in the stream, the kingcups are brighter and trout are firmer in outline.

The dry fly angler of today, unless in a pitiful state of self-sufficiency, moves pace by pace beside the mysterious deeps in company. His foot falls where others fell before. He who shelters beneath the Mottisfont oak is not alone for Hills fished the Oakley Stream. Houghton, Middleton and the upper reaches, Wherwell, too, and Bransbury Common he knew, from 1890 onwards. A long span of casting years until the second revised edition of his book in 1930 stamped his observations on that era. Then the world passed on and he was left behind. Or was he?

APRIL AND THE EARLY DAYS
If you sat beside the Oakley Stream at noon on 26 April 1990 you might feel his hand tighten in excitement on your shoulder. 'Look', he would say, pointing, 'large dark olives.' That night, at home, as a brace of brownies await attention and the frying pan, turn the pages of his book:

'I walked up, and suddenly, without preparation, unexpected and wonderful as it always is, however often you see it, the real hatch started. Olives were coming down thick, in little bands of half a dozen or so, blown together by the wind, and the trout were rising quietly and quickly and continuously, all up the river, three or four of them within reach, and good fish too. There is a quality of magic about these early spring rises.'

In Devon as in Hampshire, on Dart, Test and Taw, the large dark olives hatch at noon and not before. Other flies appear: iron blue, pale wateries and smuts. Hills adjures you to 'keep looking at the water . . . . waste no time . . . . rises begin and end suddenly.' How right he is and how happily observes 'All the best of the year is in front of you . . . .'

MAYFLY

This Hills describes as an interlude, and so it is. While still delighting in the river, I feel he did not relish the disturbance, the overpowering presence, the glut and the overshadowing of the tiny wings of lesser ephemerids by their heavy, fluttering brothers. The mayfly dominates the scene. 'Both the newly hatched and also the spent insect sometimes come down in masses which no one would believe possible who had not seen them. The water is covered, trout are not taking one fly in a hundred, your artificial has to float among droves of naturals, and there seems no imaginable reason why the fish should ever take it.'

But given the situation he shortens the odds by choosing two days out of two or three weeks: the two best days, the fourth and the twelfth day after that. On the Kennet my father-in-law, with 85 years behind him, holds off until the third. There is something in the suspicion that trout are frightened by so large a mouthful. Time, four days, is needed to overcome fear and acquire the taste. This is also true of the daddy long legs which skips across the water – he usually arrives safely at the far bank.

> 'That is the first great chance, the fourth day. And the next is the twelfth day, by which time the fly is going off and the trout know it, and are making the most of the short time remaining. They are feeding steadily on spent fly, and, moreover, the big fish who have been hooked and lost earlier have forgotten all about it and are on the move again. Your best chance of a big fish is either the fourth or the twelfth day.'

To shorten the odds still more, he uses a soft-hackled fly which he is certain takes a firmer hold. He may have been right. Stiff feather wings, or modern ones of bucktail, protect the hook from enclosing jaws. The mayfly is over and the weed cut, too, by the final week of June. Our passionate expectations, exhausted in duffer's fortnight, are at a low level. Anglers no longer hurry to the river for eighteen hours of daylight separate the twilight hours. Now are the weeks when we sit and watch and plot the downfall of individual trout. Dry fly men are confidence tricksters. To deceive high summer trout, single fish, the Harrys, Freds and Charlies who survived the mayfly, exercises us. So, we sit on the bench beside the water and watch. We almost qualify to be the subject of that most irritating remark 'You must be very patient'. If I had an umbrella I dare say I would sit under it and fall asleep with one eye open for a rise. Trout too take their time. Of the Test in June Hills writes:

> 'The cast was made, and by the mercy of fate the fly for once landed
> just right. There it was, floating gaily in the slack water, cocked, and
> the line behind it was beautifully crooked to absorb the drag. And there
> too was the trout, slowly turning himself out to look at it. He came
> out, raised his nose to it, and for what seemed an eternity backed down
> behind it as the stream carried it along; then he broke the water and
> took it. Once more I had the fortitude to wait until his head was well
> down again, indeed until he had turned to go back, before striking. I
> knew then I had him firm.'

Isn't that delightful? Time to count the spots on his flank, see his eye locked onto the fly and know you are about to win the battle of wits and wiles – unless he turns away!

> 'July is the month of the evening rise. No fishing is so disappointing.'

Even so, Hills is sustained throughout the day by the picture of last light, of a patch of shining water enclosed by darkness. In that final 30 minutes leviathans may arise to stretch their fins and disturb the silken surface of the water.

> 'But, after all, though the evening may not realise our hopes, it is ever

before us, throughout the long summer day. Spinners will fall on the water: the blue-winged olive, with its narrow wings, looking large in the twilight, will suddenly appear: we shall hear, loud in the silence, the splash of a big fellow walloping at the sedge. The heavy wind will die down with the sun . . . .'

For summer fishing, Hills is . . . .

'quite certain that it pays to carry a large variety [of flies].'

He changes frequently. If a pattern fails to tempt, off it comes and on goes something different.

'I use a large number. I have looked up in my diary three hot summer days, one each from the last three years. Trout rose at, or were landed on, eighteen different flies (I caught fourteen); eighteen, without counting large sedges used at dusk. Here are the patterns: three different nymphs, orange partridge, small red partridge, hackle blue-wing, two different sedges, smut, black ant, yellow boy, sherry spinner, Houghton ruby, ginger quill, caperer, hackle hare's ear, Lunn's Particular and orange quill. I am certain that I should not have done so well had I used two or three patterns only. I am quite certain of it.'

I have never found a fatal fly and hope I never do; a fly which warranted that over-used description 'deadly'. But Hills was very close . . . .

'You reel in, take your scissors, and clip the hackle short until there is little left except the body (often a very profitable dodge) but still he gives it nothing more than a cold, concentrated stare. What are you to do? You cannot use smaller flies. Why, try a caperer – the invaluable caperer – the greatest of the summer flies. Many and many are the fish it has yielded to me in burning, still weather, under a cloudless sky, in transparent water.'

THE WINGED CAPERER

William Lunn's dressing – first used on the Test 27 May 1917.

BODY, four or five strands from a turkey tail feather, two strands from a swan's feather dyed yellow to make a ring of yellow in the centre of the body.

WINGS, coot, bleached and dyed chocolate-brown.

HACKLE, one medium Rhode Island cock hackle, one black cock hackle put on in front of wings.

TYING SILK, Pearsall's gossamer No. 13

HOOK, 1 to 2

Note – bleach the coot's feather in peroxide.

But the year draws on . . . .

'There is nothing very special to be said about September fishing, except that it is very good.'

I agree with Hills, the excellence of September is a fact. So also are the equinox, the gales and the rain of that month. Disturbances are a blessing. Blessed also is a gentle warm rain, that encourager of the generous hatch of fly, provider of the West Country spate and replenisher of the failing Hampshire spring. 'If I go fishing to catch trout, give me a wet day', wrote Oliver Kite in the 1960s, and while married to the upper Avon.

When rain ceases hatches start and Hills is at the river. 'By now the sun had come out and so had the duns. There was a nice, steady, even hatch from eleven to three. I got two more fish . . . .'

But his conscience is not at ease, for the time of the redd draws nigh. That is the trouble with September, the arrival of the final days when few fishing hours remain. The river sucks you close in its magnetic field but the thought of gravid trout repels. Hills is in two minds: 'Even on the Test, moreover, most of those you take you can quite well keep.' A page later his doubts surface: '. . . . a picture very different from that of May. And the trout are different too. It must be confessed that they are easier. But they do not get really easy until the poor brutes are slack and out of condition and then, of course, they should be left alone.'

THE EVENING RISE

'. . . . when the great red sedge is flopping about in his feeble and aimless flight, and clouds of smaller sedges are flickering tirelessly up and down over the unbroken surface, perchance some dim memory begins to stir in the slow mind of the old trout. All the season through he has fed at the bottom, grubbing on shrimps and caddis and water-snails and minnows and even on his relatives. But he recalls seasons such as this, far back in former years, when all was quiet and warm and peaceful, when fat sedges would tumble clumsily on to the water, and in their efforts to escape would make a ripple and commotion spreading far over the placid pool, and he remembers how fresh and fair they were to eat. Then he forsakes his lair under the arched willow roots and rises to the top and takes up his old station in the shadow of the tussock, where he used to lie long ago in his active middle age, when he weighed a bare two pounds. Aye, he weighs more than twice two pounds now, perhaps three times or more, he is the prize of a lifetime – and perhaps as your sedge comes over him you will see a break like that of a big raindrop, a little circle like that of the palm of a man's hand, and when you strike you will think you have hooked the trunk of a tree.'

Mottisfont Abbey Estate

RALPH COLLINS — TROUT KEEPER
31 AUGUST 1989

I MET RALPH at 9.30 am 100 yards above Main Bridge, which is the lower boundary of his water. He was standing in a square boat, not readily rowable, but designed for his purpose. Bolted to the bows was an iron ring, 6 inches in diameter, through which he had thrust a pole into the river bed. From this stationary platform the Mottisfont keeper was cutting weed with a pole scythe, this being the final day of the August cut. The boat rocked as he worked, sending waves across the river. His beat is wide; a long cast would cover half the width.

> 'I always leave this bit until the last day of my cut; from the car park under the willows to the bridge. I can do that in a day, the whole lot of it if I get a move on. Anyone'll tell you I can get a move on when cutting weed. It's hard work, but I can do it. I enjoy it. I can fother-on all day and be out by tea time. Do you know what? It's taken me last week and this week to get the river in order. You see this weed – that's what we call lamb's tail which will cut like a piece of cake. It's good weed. I leave some in the middle to break the river into two flows. This year it'll take longer due to this blanket weed clogging my scythe. Fertilizers off the land make it grow, and the shortage of water. We were short of water in '76, but the blanket weed wasn't so bad because there was less nitrogen fertilizer. I've never known a year like this one. It was bad in '76 but I didn't have the difficulty in cutting weed that I've got now.'

The Mottisfont Estate is owned by the National Trust who let the river to Marley Tiles. 'You know, Sir Owen Aisher. He's had it for 34 years. He's 89 years of age and still fishes every week. He's retired. I've worked for him personally for 15 years, and for Marley. We've about $1\frac{1}{2}$ miles on the big river and many streams as well. No rods are let; the river is fished by his friends.'

Ralph's father worked on the estate for 44 years. 'He told me that there was a job going on the river under Bert Pragnall, the head keeper. We worked together to begin with for a number of years. I work by myself now.'

Today there are a greater number of fishermen than in the old days and Ralph stocks the river with browns of about $1\frac{1}{2}$ to 2 lb. These are obtained from Mick Lunn at Stockbridge. Fingerlings go in each year and wild fish are caught as a result. If he puts in rainbows they are introduced in the dog days of July.

'I spend quite a lot of my time with the fishermen, setting them up and sorting them out.' Two arrived as we talked, Mr Bissett and Mr Jenner, who had been coming to the river for 20 years. They are friends of Sir Owen and fish annually at Mottisfont. 'They are good fishermen. They'll take a brace each.'

Salmon spawn on the estate, but not as many as in the days of Bert Pragnall. During the fishing season one is lucky to see a salmon break the surface. At one time they caught half a dozen on salmon flies in a season, but today to fish for them would be a waste of time.

Mick Lunn does Ralph's electric fishing once a year, at the end of the season. They pick up about half-a-dozen pike. Years ago they would have stunned 20. The largest he has taken weighed 22 lb. They turned-up three on that day; the other two weighed 12 lb each. Recently they have all been small. In addition to electric fishing Ralph snares them with a wire on a pole, and catches a few spinning in the winter with a copper spoon. Pike traps are placed in the feeder streams where they go to spawn. He takes out grayling as well, but not to denude the water, for he likes to see them rise.

We sat on a bench beside the river that morning at 10 am. Olives hatched. A trout rose far out. 'A rainbow. A little one. He's an escapee from the fish farm down below. We caught crayfish in the old days, in traps on the Abbey stretch. Bert Pragnall took them in Grig Pots, designed for the job. Mr Russell asked for them. He liked crayfish, and owned the Abbey.'

Two years ago they had an invasion of 200 hippies. They swam naked in Ralph's river, 70 at a time. 'You saw a bit of nature.' The police chased them, but when they were cleared off one end they jumped in at the other. Old vans and buses were their transport. 'I had to close the river to the fishermen for a fortnight. They weren't a violent lot, but I got a bit of abuse.'

We drove in Ralph's van towards his house, crossing a stream named the Rectory on the way, and then on to the Oakley fishing hut. There, close to the river, is an oak tree. Mentioned in *Domesday Book*, the tree is huge, the base of the trunk as wide as a Rolls is long. A cow calved inside the

Mottisfont. Head keeper Ralph Collins clearing blanket weed from his scythe.

133

hollow trunk at the turn of the century. As I photographed the tree a barn owl flew out of a hole in the trunk – a hole streaked with white droppings. A little owl then flew in to the claw-like branches. Many pheasants rustled in the dry undergrowth. Later, when I met Mrs Collins, she told me that her grandmother, who was born in 1894 and died aged 92, remembered playing inside the tree as a child.

The thatched Oakley hut stands beside the river, and there Ralph prepares lunch on Fridays for Sir Owen. Inside, in the gloom, two cased brown trout hang on the walls. One is large, 'All of 5 lb', said Ralph. The other is small and deformed, a curiosity, being swollen like a bullfrog forward of the dorsal fin. The large trout was caught before the days of stocking and must be 70 years old. It was landed in the time of a river-keeper named Coxen, whose son, aged 94, is still alive. The hut is in a glade, 20 feet from the running water, surrounded and covered by roses.

The river has a bed of clear gravel, well suited to natural spawning, but that August, due to drought, the level of the water was depressed. I glanced at a water level hole beneath a tree trunk revealed by the sunken stream. Ralph caught my eye and commented that he had not seen an otter there for 16 years.

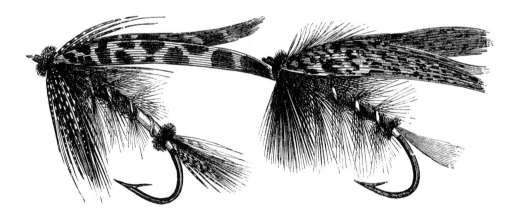

OPPOSITE *Mottisfont, The Oakley Hut.*

On the way to his cottage we passed the Oakley farmhouse which nestles by the river; you could catch a trout from the back door. Outside the cottage flows the Dun, a stream which starts at Alderbury, not far from Salisbury. It runs down through West Dean, Lockerley and Dunbridge, picking up water from springs all the way, before joining the Test at Kimbridge. A stream of many whirling holes where trout may lie beneath the washed-out roots of trees. We lay on the floor of his living room where he spread out the estate fishing records of which I record the 1984 season:

TOTAL FISH	405	
BROWN	155	
RAINBOW	250	
OAKLEY STREAM	Brown	36
	Rainbow	62
RECTORY STREAM	Brown	52
	Rainbow	60
MAIN	Brown	67
	Rainbow	128
TOTAL WEIGHT	1033 lb 6 oz	
AVERAGE WEIGHT	Brown	2 lb 6 oz
	Rainbow	2 lb $10\frac{1}{2}$ oz
BEST BROWN	3 lb 8 oz	
BEST RAINBOW	5 lb	

39 fish over 3 lb
8 fish over 4 lb
4 fish over 5 lb

I took away with me the impression of a rugged countryman, a Test keeper by right of experience, wise in the ways of the river. Strong as oak, he is proud of his work and his life amidst the wild creatures, the willows, the trout, and the water buttercups of the valley.

OPPOSITE *Broadlands House.*

Kimbridge

JIM HADDRELL – TROUT FISHING INSTRUCTOR
6 MARCH 1989

I MET JIM HADDRELL at the Orvis shop in the High Street of Stockbridge, centre of trout fishing on the Test. Many anglers have started dry fly chalk stream angling with his help. Jim dispenses knowledge, humour, fairy tales, coffee and gems of trouting wisdom from his waterside wooden hut on the river bank. His personality at once emerged 'You go fishing for fun. If a thing's worth doing it's worth doing badly, so long as you're enjoying it. Come on, let's go to the river. You follow my Land Rover in that MG hip bath of yours.' So saying, he shot through the door, ground the engine of the Land Rover to life, stirred the gear lever into place, and bounced down the bumpy road on hard springs to Kimbridge. I followed him to his secret park, a clearing in the trees and shrubs within earshot of the running river.

While we waited for the electric fishing boat to arrive with John Mullins, Southern Water head bailiff, Jim talked. He is good at talking and therein lies the secret of his success as an instructor. 'The thing in teaching is to find out what makes a pupil relax.' He rarely has a failure.

Jim was born in Wiltshire, outside Calne, and chose an army career. At 60 years of age he took up trout fishing, joining the Services Fly Fishing Association on the river Avon. The first season he failed to catch a fish, 'but my dog stole a trout from someone else'. He then read Oliver Kite's book *Nymph Fishing in Practice*. That first winter, from October to December, he fished the nymph at Bulford until he could 'catch grayling with my eyes closed'. He then read a second book, written by a brigadier. The brigadier commented on Jim's performance: 'Hrmph, hrmph. In the good old days before the water was flogged – rhubarb, rhubarb, hrmph, hrmph. I have only known four fishermen who have taken 100 fish out of that stretch in a season.' Jim had 102 fish on the bank by July. 'Half the members thought I was wonderful. The other half hated my guts. I stopped fishing.'

He teaches casting in the traditional overhead style, standing upright, facing straight forward. When executing the forward cast his body bends from the waist in what he describes as 'the aristocratic stoop'. He has, unwittingly, so described his method to incognito earls.

The trans-Atlantic link with Orvis brought an American author to the Ginger Beer beat. Water foams and bubbles out of the sluices at the neck of this stretch, and tall mealies grow close behind the bank. By lunchtime Jim had tied on about 40 tippets for the angler who caught his fly in the corn cobs on the back cast every time.

Jim: 'I suppose the corn in the USA doesn't grow so tall as ours.'

American: 'That's a stupid remark. What would you do?'

Jim: 'Well, I'm bone idle. I'd sit down for a while and watch. Then pick up my rod like this and cast once to a fish and catch it.' And he did!

GINGER BEER BEAT

The Ginger Beer beat is $\frac{1}{3}$ mile in length. As there are shallows at the downstream end of his water the beat retains the 2 lb browns which are stocked and obtained from Mick Lunn at Houghton. In addition, roaming rainbows, a free issue, drop down-river into his beat. He does not put in large fish, but it is rare for a season to pass without someone taking a 10 lb brown which has grown in the wild. His fishermen usually have these mounted.

'A couple of years ago a client caught a 2 lb grayling. "Must have it mounted", he said. I sent it to the taxidermist. Three or four weeks later the taxidermist telephoned. He was in a dreadful state. He had taken the grayling out of the deep freeze to thaw, but whilst absent, having a cup of coffee, his dog ate the fish. "What shall I do?". I told him "Stuff the dog".' Jim solved the problem. He went to the river, caught two grayling and sent them off, 'one for stuffing and one for the dog'.

He is certain the secret of success in trout-catching lies in the use of fine nylon, the tip of which should never be greased. 'I like to go to the river, spot a fish, and say "that's the fish I'm going to have", and take him first cast.' Sometimes he ties on a bare hook with a twist of copper wire 'like Ollie Kite'. It was clear to me that Jim does not fish the water – he goes for individual trout. He thinks and plots their downfall. As he says, 'In fishing and shooting, if you're not getting anything, you should adjust the nut at the butt end.'

ELECTRIC FISHING

We were joined at the riverside hut by John Mullins, and Ian Spiller, the Southern Water bailiff from the river Meon. John is a busy man, much occupied with electric fishing in early spring and autumn at which times poaching surveillance has to take second place. Poachers are again busy in the winter, sneaking spawning salmon in the Winchester and Romsey areas of the Itchen and the Test. Between Christmas and early January he catches-up salmon to strip the eggs. February and March are river management months, and then the poaching starts again in the spring when salmon come in from the sea. To tackle poachers they agreed that body weight was useful, but Jim believes in equalizers 'like big sticks, and getting in the first blow'. Southern Water bailiffs are told that poachers must have first crack, but Jim will not accept this disadvantage. He put a notice in the rear window of his car, 'Before you break in to this car get yourself measured for a wheel chair, and telephone for an ambulance. I am well known for Grieveous Bodily Harm.' The car has never been touched.

We unloaded the dinghy from the trailer and slid the boat into the water. I was warned that the 500-volt current is lethal; Jim thus decided to use my cameras from the bank while I helped in the boat.

The operation then started. The cathode is a bunch of 3-foot-long tentacles which trail in the water. In the bows of the boat are two electric probes and their operators. The probes, on the end of wooden shafts, are metal hoops 18 inches in diameter which are held beneath the surface and swept from side to side upstream of the boat. These probes have a finger switch in the handle which cuts the current if finger pressure is released. To the rear of the probe operators are two netsmen who scoop out coarse fish and drop them into a water-filled dustbin in the bottom of the boat. In the stern is a generator, and the helmsman who operates the outboard motor.

With the current off, we drifted the boat down to the lower end of the beat, then switched on and worked up-river. In this manner stunned trout, which are not netted, are carried away downstream by the water flow, out of the electric field. They recover and dart off into the depths with no apparent discomfort.

The netsmen have to be quick and alert to spot submerged, stunned fish and eels, and trap them before they drift away and the boat moves on. We took about 50 grayling, a 6 inch gudgeon and 2 gravid female perch, a rarity in these waters. The perch were removed for breeding. No pike surfaced but we gained a sackful of squirming eels. On the bank the grayling were put in large water-filled dustbins for transport to coarse fishing waters, while the eels were set aside for John Russell, Orvis' Managing Director. Jim also catches eels from the bank with a weighted hook and a piece of trout offal as bait. He hangs them on a sharp nail driven through the wooden side of his hut, slits the skin behind the head and peels it down.

OPPOSITE *Electric fishing for coarse fish. A probe is at each end of the boat which holds an electric generator. Netsman in centre to lift out stunned fish.*

Kimbridge Estate

IAN VEAL — SPORTING MANAGER
1 FEBRUARY 1989

Iʌɴ sᴛᴀʀᴛᴇᴅ ʀɪᴠᴇʀ ᴡᴏʀᴋ as a keeper for Lord and Lady Graham at King-fisher Lodge on the Itchen. After five years he came to Kimbridge following the death of the previous head-keeper, Les Vane. Ian came to the estate in 1971 and is still there. 'People like Bernard Aldrich and myself learned our craft on the river, we read books and I have attended all the Two Lakes conferences. Travel has broadened my experience: to Denmark, the States and other places abroad connected with fishing.'

The fishery has $5\frac{1}{2}$ miles of bank on both sides of the main river, one mile of the river Dun, and a four-acre lake. The lower limit of the fishery is the bridge at Kimbridge, and the upper end is the Mottisfont bridge.

Season rods each have 30 days' fishing and may take them when they wish. Ian divides the rods between those who are retired, who are able to fish mid-week, and those in full employment who are free only at week-ends. There is a long waiting list and, to ensure a happy team, replacements are filled on the basis of 'Friend of a friend and dead man's shoes'. At the same time the fishing is not limited to the season team. Each year they try to find a few people who have never fished the river; they are offered two or three days free fishing, usually in the evening, in July and August. In July 1989 they organized an event called Commonwealth Fly Fishers, which had been held in the central highlands of Tasmania in 1988. The day was 'catch and release'. 'During the day they caught very little on dry fly. Becoming frustrated they asked to fish the nymph. I refused. In the evening it all came right, there was a great rise and they had a bonanza. They stayed in the fishing lodge by the river. We call the lodge Mill Cottage. Originally it was in two halves: one for the chauffeur and the gardener occupied the other. Mr and Mrs Arthur Humbert (page 144) lived there until about 1977 before moving to Kimbridge farmhouse.'

The stocking is 85% brown trout and 15% rainbows. Trout do not breed

142

naturally at this lower end of the river due to methane gas rising through the river bed which kills the alevins at the yolk sac stage. To overcome this problem Ian introduces between 15 and 20,000 fry each year. The stocking with takable fish is not done at set times. 'We stock as required. This makes us walk the river. We see the state of things: fly life, the banks and how the weed is growing.' Weed cutting takes place at the usual agreed dates. Much of the river, being deep, is cut with the weed cutting boat. The banks are trimmed and fringes topped, but all wild flowers are left.

It was clear that Ian wished to reduce disturbance in the valley for the benefit of wildlife. 'I had a little pond dug for salmon parr. It proved unsuitable and became derelict. I gave permission to someone to put in some crested newts on the condition "that you do not come back to look at them. Leave them alone. Nature will look after them." It's the same with the RSPB and nest boxes – they put them up and then keep coming back to see who is inside.'

Ian is keen to impart knowledge of the countryside, 'You can talk to the children who come to see the fishery and the fish farm, and educate them in the ways of the river. Some of them have a go with a worm in the winter, to get them going and enthusiastic.'

Ian takes a long view of the state of the river and the valley; the effects of UDN, water abstraction, pollution and wildlife populations.

'If anything went wrong with the Test there would be such a hue and cry from the keepers that the situation would be immediately remarked. Life is a cycle which man sometimes interrupts, but solutions are found. So long as we are sensible and don't do stupid things, the Test will be here for ever. The woods, the fields, the river and the valley. Many people love these things. If a thing goes wrong, within 20 years it will be corrected by the cycle.'

Kimbridge

THE HUMBERTS — FISHING RECORDS
24 OCTOBER 1989

Arthur Humbert opened the door of Kimbridge farm house at 8.55 am. 'I'm very glad you're early. Come in. Will you have tea or coffee?' In the study I was motioned to a chair in front of a partner's desk. Arthur sat behind, upright and prepared. On the desk, waiting, were three leather-bound fishing diaries – the estate records. Arthur started: 'Now', he said, 'I want to give you all the help I can. It is many years since a record was made of the fishing on the Test. High time it was undertaken. You have a difficult task.'

19 May 1934. Arthur's father, Charles, took a trout of 5 lb 6 oz from the Mill Cottage lawn; the largest trout caught on the Kimbridge water since 1900. It was 22 in long with a girth of $13\frac{3}{4}$ in. 'Such fish lived near mills. They took their summer holiday in May, going out to feed on mayfly. For the other 49 weeks they fed on mice which dropped from the miller's floor, and all sorts of things like that.'

Reproduced in the estate diaries is the record Arthur's father made of fish caught between 1900 and 1912. It is noted that in 1900 his great uncle caught 26 grayling at an average weight of 1 lb 14 oz. The stocking of trout in those years is recorded:

In 1903, 25,000 eyed ova and 1000 yearlings.

1905, 15,000 eyed ova. All this stocking evidently did very little good.

In 1906 a grayling 3 lb 0 oz killed by A.H.

In 1910 home-grown three-year-olds were stocked: the result is obvious from the large increase in the bag, and A. N. Gilbey caught the largest trout of 3 lb 2 oz.

Arthur continued:

'The statistics from 1900 to 1909 show an average of 82 trout per annum. For 1910 to 1912 the catch rose to 367 per annum with the

144

introduction of home-grown three-year-olds. This is a very good illustration of why you need to stock the Test. In my youth there were always a few very large roach, perch and masses of pike. It is the intervention of man that has made it what it now is – a trout fishery. Certainly, below Kimbridge, there is a stretch of water which, left to its own, would rapidly revert to pike. In those years, 1900 to 1910, when there were many coarse fish, the small fry and yearlings introduced were gobbled up by coarse fish. More importantly, there are few shallows in the middle Test, few spawning beds, and the water is such that very young fish do not do well. In fact, today, at our trout farm, we find it best to buy in our little fish at weights where 100 weigh 1 lb. They are little matchsticks.'

We studied the 1928 diary entries 'What this shows is that the fishing was mostly during the mayfly, and little later on.' A fish was caught on 15 April, and then nothing until May. Then $8\frac{1}{4}$ pages of the diary up to 6 June, but only $2\frac{1}{2}$ pages from then until the end of the season. 12 fish are on each page, there being a separate line for each. 'In 1928 my great uncle was not well. Perhaps a smaller number of guests were invited. This may have resulted in over-emphasis of the mayfly/rest of the season division.'

We looked at 1921, a drought year, and moved on to 1923. This showed a season of 348 trout at an average weight of 1 lb 10 oz. 'The rods would have been friends of the family – no rods were let.' There was 1 page for April, 16 pages up to 7 June and then 4 pages for the rest of the season with the final entry on 21 September.

I chose a page: 19 July to 4 August. The flies on which the trout recorded had been caught were:

Kimbridge Sedge Tup
Blue Quill (2 fish) Kimbridge Sedge
Houghton Ruby Black Ant
Blue Quill (2 fish) Blue Quill
Black Ant (2 fish)

The 12 flies equalling the 12 lines on the page.

Who were the rods fishing the estate waters at that time? We turned to the first page of 1924, and followed that year through. Peter and E. B. C. Curtis, (a local family in those days), Eroll Sprick, F. H. Taylor (relation), C. B. Williams (relation), Cecil Baker (the factor on Compton Manor which was owned by his sister). Col. Langford, Cdr. Llewellyn. The flies on 18 May were

Olive (4 fish)	Blue Quill
Blue Quill (2 fish)	Mayfly
Greenwell	Mayfly
Mayfly	Blue Quill

There were notable catches on 24 May:
Sir Roger Gregory took 9 trout. 2 lb, 2 lb, 1 lb 14 oz, 1 lb 15 oz, 3 lb 7 oz, 1 lb 7 oz, 1 lb 4 oz, 1 lb 14 oz.
Mrs Humbert (Arthur's great-uncle's wife) caught 3 fish.
On 26 May C. E. Pain, who wrote *Fifty Years on the Test*, 1934, set about the river with a mayfly, 'He must have been a very skilled angler', 1 lb 9 oz, 1 lb 8 oz, 1 lb 8 oz, 2 lb 3 oz, 3 lb 4 oz, 1 lb 11 oz, 2 lb, 3 lb 10 oz, all with a north-west wind.
The 1924 total was 384 trout weighing 688 lb, an average of 1 lb 13 oz. Today the average is about $2\frac{1}{2}$ lb.

I asked about the family connection with Kimbridge. 'My great-uncle, Arthur Humbert, after whom I was christened in the hope that he might leave me something, but he never did, bought the miller's house at the end of the 1800s. In those days the mill ground corn; today only the old water wheel remains to generate 2 Kw of electricity.' The structure of the mill is recorded in the 1900 photograph. The mill has gone. In its place are a workshop, a garage and a cottage built in 1906.

'Don't ask me what he paid for the mill – I'd love to know. But I can tell you that in 1913 he paid 200 guineas for a pair of Holland & Holland 12 bores. In 1934 he died and my father, Charles, bought the estate. It was during the agricultural depression and a year of drought. My father understood it had been left to him, but when the will was opened it was found to have been left elsewhere. He had to buy it. The estate was put on the market at the proper time, in early May but, because of the drought the river looked terrible, and I daresay he left the weeds uncut to make it look a bit worse, because he was managing the place. He bought it at the end of October when the executors had withdrawn it from the market. It rained that day!'

The actual purchase comprised 4 acres. Since then there have been 13 more purchases to make 360 acres and $5\frac{1}{2}$ miles of fishing bank. There are 2 keepers today, as there were during the inter-war years. Standards have been maintained and improved by mechanization. The fishing now gives pleasure to a great many more people than in the old days.

We looked at a picture brought into the study by Anne. Entitled *Valley of the Test*, the river wound into the distance; the banks bare; there were no trees other than a few some way from the water. The method of fishing was the reason. A wind was required to assist 'blowing'. Today, all the trees are younger than 100 years. 'In those days the owners of cart horses earned a few extra bob on still, windless days when anglers fished from their backs to obtain extra height for their blow lines. In 1936 I helped

The valley of the Test in the 1830s. The trees have been cut down to allow plenty of wind for the blow-line.

my father plant poplars on the river. There are many more trees now than 100 years ago.' Anne showed me photographs taken in 1928 of the treeless course of the Dun or Lockerly Stream at Kimbridge. In 1983 she had identified the sites and taken the same scenes to show many extra trunks and increased vegetation.

I asked Arthur to describe his ideal fishing day. With no hesitation he replied:

'I would choose September, the second week, a warm still evening without mist, the third evening after rain. I would fish from the left bank to catch the sunset; late in the evening with the sun in front of me. I would use a Red Sedge. If you'd like to bring along a half-bottle of champagne and a small pot of caviar we could really write them off.'

The Mill, Kimbridge, in c 1900. Now replaced by a workshop, garage and cottage, but the river bridges to the rear of the wagon survive.

148

Kimbridge

MILL COTTAGE

I AN VEAL TOOK ME ACROSS the farmhouse lawn, over the Test, and we entered Mill Cottage which stands beside the mill pool. Open the door to step into a combined dining and sitting room. On the walls are paintings of birds, tales of the capture of many fish, poems and cased trout, portly in their dimensions. One, with a spray of dried hops as a frieze on top of the case and a Kimbridge Sedge enclosed, read:

> 5 lbs. Killed at Kimbridge by C.H. on 30th May 1936.
> Length $21\frac{1}{8}$. Girth $13\frac{7}{8}$. Length of head $4\frac{1}{2}$

There was also the framed account of:

A DAY WHEN EVERYTHING WENT RIGHT
Kimbridge No 2 Beat. May 28. 1928.
This cast and fly landed 13 trout and 4 grayling. The cast (Hardy's tapered to 3 X) used for the third day. The fly had been used one previous day.
Weights:
13 trout. 4-5, 3-10, 2-7, 1-12, 1-9, 1-8, 1-8 (killed)
6 between $1\frac{1}{2}$ and 1 lb returned
4 grayling 1-10, 1-10, 1-2, 1-0,
Total weight $29\frac{3}{4}$ lb.
There were not a great quantity of fish rising but almost every fish thrown at was landed. The best fish (4 lb 5 oz) killed opposite the garden, the last cast of a perfect holiday.
Weather: bright, hot, no wind.

Before leaving Mill Cottage I sat at the dining table to copy a framed poem hanging on a wall. I do not think I am alone in having prayed for assistance at the waterside.

Late in the second week of May
when May-fly take their holiday
Tired of pursuing lesser fry
I sallied forth resolved to try
For one of those great super trout
that Alf had recently put out.
Soon I found one, there he lay
under a tussock in a bay,
Like a great liner in the stream
nine inches draught, six inches beam;
Watching in wonderment and awe
the largest trout I ever saw,
I spoke aloud a foolish wish,
'I'd sell my soul to catch that fish.'
I'd hardly spoken when I spied
a total stranger at my side,
Who said 'If that's the way you feel
I'm quite prepared to do a deal,
My name, Sir, is Beelzebub
tho' not a member of your club
Amongst you I have lately found
a promising recruiting ground.
The younger folk I tempt to Hades
with cocktails, cards and pretty ladies,
But when it comes to older members
whose vital fires have sunk to embers
Failing inducement of the flesh
I have to think of something fresh
Whereby the older members can
(provided they're prepared to sign
This form upon the dotted line)
catch anything they care to fish for
What more can these old busters wish for?

I think you'll find it worth your while
To give my scheme a little trial.'
Now from the corner of my eye
I'd seen some May-fly floating by
so shouting 'Down Sir, your help's not needed'
I hooked him, but was promptly weeded.
I slackened line, I pulled it tight,
From right to left, from left to right;
T'was shortly clear I might as well
Have hooked the Grosvenor Hotel.
Beelzebub, who all the while
Had watched with an indulgent smile,
said, 'So he's weeded you the bounder!
He looked about a seven pounder,
perhaps in view of this resistance
May now I offer my assistance?'
and with a merry little caper
He proffered me a pen and paper.
Seized with desire, to conscience blind,
I took the fountain pen and signed,
When prompted by some devilish urge
I saw Leviathan emerge
and sail serenely alongside
Like Queen Mary on the tide
And here I must admit that Nick
Was both resourceful, cute and quick
for stooping low above the whale
he gaffed the monster with his tail
remarking as he wiped the sting
'This is a handy little thing,
and now, Sir, let me shake your hand
As one of our devoted band.
We'll give you in a year or so
A nice warm welcome down below,
meanwhile it's been a fruitful stroll
You've caught your fish, I've caught my soul.

Ha-ha, excuse my little joke!
He gave my ribs a playful poke
and in a panic I awoke.

St Andrew's Church, Timsbury.

Timsbury

IVOR MASON
24 OCTOBER 1989

IVOR MASON LIVES close to St Andrew's Church in the small hamlet of Timsbury. Ivor Mason is not a keeper, but is intimately connected with the river as a fishery maintenance contractor. He has a Land Rover, a tractor, and electric fishing and weed cutting boats. He talked with me in his house and then we went to the river, to the Club's new fishing hut.

> 'I first came to Timsbury 14 years ago to work for Mr Ben Halpin, one of the river owners. He's dead now. At present I look after the Club waters which have been much reduced in recent years. Two beats on the main river were sold, together with three beats on the carrier. Three miles of bank are left to the owner, Mr Nick Oppenheim. I look after the weed cutting and the banks. Last week we electric fished, taking out two pike of 19 lb and 12 lb. Last year we didn't catch one, but ten years ago a pike of $37\frac{1}{2}$ lb was taken on live bait.'

Fishing on the four beats is by a rotating system for the members, who number in the region of 28. The Club buy in brown and rainbow trout to stock straight into the river, rainbows predominating at the end of the season. There is no salmon fishing further upstream than Timsbury, but Ivor thought that none had been caught on the Club waters in 1989. I asked his opinion of the condition of the river: 'Over the years there has been a lot more silt and rubbish coming down, and a great deal more blanket weed. When I'm using my weed cutting boat these days I cannot really cut because of the blanket weed. I just sort of push it all along, even though my boat has both vertical and horizontal reciprocating blades.'

Ivor's two great-nephews Stuart and Wayne Morgan, were staying with him during the school half-term. Stuart told me 'When I grow up I'm going to be a keeper.'

Salmon on The Test

JOHN POTTER — THE SALMON REHABILITATION
PROGRAMME
5 JULY 1989

I ASKED JOHN, who is chairman of the Test and Itchen Fishing Association, about the salmon scene on the Test, the decline in numbers and the re-stocking scheme.

'I think we have seen a decline in the salmon catches on the Test for a long time, since the late 1950s. Whether there is also a decline in the run is another matter, but there probably is a decline.'

To illustrate the reduction in salmon grassed over the years, and in support of John's suspicions I give below the catches at Nursling for the period 1932 to 1968 together with the last two full seasons.

	LITTLE RIVER	MAIN RIVER	TOTAL		LITTLE RIVER	MAIN RIVER	TOTAL
1932	282	234	516	1947	144	7	151
1933	315	120	435	1948	226	48	274
1934	418	129	547	1949	304	34	338
1935	399	161	560	1950	313	29	342
1936	220	118	338	1951	252	38	290
1937	236	93	329	1952	345	56	401
1938	289	18	307	1953	368	146	514
1939	306	114	420	1954	610	248	858
1940	263	55	318	1955	301	171	472
1941	283	127	410	1956	445	106	551
1942	514	38	552	1957	309	77	386
1943	572	92	664	1958	407	195	602
1944	534	53	587	1959	358	141	499
1945	210	20	230	1960	320	117	437
1946	198	4	202	1961	211	109	320

	LITTLE RIVER	MAIN RIVER	TOTAL		LITTLE RIVER	MAIN RIVER	TOTAL
1962	524	186	710	1967	293	38	331
1963	373	268	641	1968	294	54	348
1964	262	100	362	1988			188
1965	407	96	503	1989			157
1966	243	75	318				

The average catch for Nursling in the 37 years from 1932 to 1968 was 434 per annum. When shall we see catches of that order again?

In answer to that question John replied:

'One keeps hoping this is a natural cycle, because many animal populations build up to a peak and then crash to a low. On the Test, if you draw a line through the highs and lows you see a steady decline. After the war there was a serious fall in salmon catches. This was followed by a population explosion which peaked in 1954. Since that year the catch has gradually slipped. We had to do something. We were advised that stocking was a process of last resort. Then along comes Southern Water, with the Ministry, and say they want to do a micro-tagging experiment, a fairly small one, with smolts. We found that we could get a return, and we thought the time had come to expand that a little bit. There has been a change from spring to late summer running. The only way, we thought, to encourage the return of the spring run was to introduce a stock that was definitely multi-sea-winter. The basis of the scheme is to re-establish the spring run. The stocking is only a part of the whole. Whether we shall succeed is anybody's guess. The fish we got from Alan Mann are all of multi-sea-winter stock. We put in 20,000 this spring.'

He went on:

'The Ministry appear to be finding that Test salmon are of different genetic make-up to salmon from Wales, the north-east, north-west and

Scotland. The 20,000 smolts introduced were of Scottish origin, totally different from Test fish – it may be found that they inter-breed with Test fish and there will be a genetic push of the progeny to multi-sea-winter. They may, on the other hand, self-destruct if the Test conditions do not suit them. Alan is also producing Test grilse eggs this year, as he has some of our own stock up in Ullapool, and we will be able to put in an equal number of these, micro-tagged.'

I asked him to explain further the rehabilitation scheme.

'What we are really after at the moment, in the stocking, micro-tagging, fish counters, young stock surveys and proposed radio-tracking, is not primarily to build up the catches, but to find out what the situation is and to pinpoint what, if anything, is going wrong – then we may be able to do something to help. It is no good starting out on haphazard schemes until we have the information on which to base sensible actions. Find out the problems : are they within or without the river? We do not yet know what has caused the decline. There have been changes up and down the river : in keepering, fish farms, water abstraction and sewage input. These may have caused deterioration – we must find out.'

On the salmon *v* trout controversy :

'There was a gentleman's agreement that salmon stopped at Romsey. This was because trout were self-generating and it was held that salmon parr competed with young trout. In fact it has now been shown in the laboratory that a young trout will see off a salmon parr. In the past salmon were treated as vermin : today they are not persecuted. But, each spring, the river is stocked with large trout. We looked at trout guts to see if there were any small salmon inside, but we could only get hold of trout caught on fly. If you could examine stomach contents at a time when alevins are hatching a different story might be revealed. What we do know is that in the Little River at Nursling in the spring of 1988, when we put in 7500 or so young fish, we caught a brown trout of about 3 lb a couple of days later that took a salmon bait. Inside this trout were five micro-tagged smolts – so war was declared on trout in the Little River by any means available. Mick Lunn says "They don't do any harm", but I take leave to differ with him.'

John explained that the 7500 little fish were not Alan Mann's – they came from Sparsholt. They were about 6 in long, smaller than natural smolts. Food supply on the Test is good, and as a result parr tend to smolt after one rather than two years.

As our conversation continued it became clear that the stocking programme was not designed to be the great saviour of salmon catches. It is more important to find out what is going on by micro-tagging the smolts, and what is happening off the Faroes and Greenland, 'Where they get a good look at the catch!' In John's opinion two things would help salmon around the British Isles: persuade Denmark to find some other method of paying for the Faroes than salmon catching; the other, to close down our own nets – 'No-one is going to help us much until we do that.' As to Denmark, they are not very keen to close down their activities 'If you find a gold mine outside your back door, you go out and work it!'

He continued 'A factor which has helped is the increase in salmon farming which has held the price steady for the last five years. Inflation has done its work on the nets which are now more amenable to selling. We must kill off the nets, particularly off Northumberland.'

We then discussed radio-tracking which John had come across on the Spey some years ago. Salmon are taken from the nets, anaesthetized, and down their throats is inserted a little radio transmitter. They are then sent on their way upstream, each giving off an identifiable 'bleep'. One was followed by a scientist all the way up the river to Grantown 'It then decided river life was not for him, went down river, and disappeared into the Moray Firth.' One or two were caught. Funny things have happened: the scientist became very excited one day when driving past the Craigellachie Hotel from which a faint 'bleep' emerged – the fish was traced to the hotel's deep freeze. This year they put a large yellow flash on the dorsal fin which says 'Oi – I've got something inside and want it saved.'

The Spey scientist found that if salmon are not caught within a fairly short space of time after entering the river they are not caught until the back-end, when they seem to wake up. In mid-journey they enter a comatose state; not many half-red fish are caught. This year (1989), a significant number went up as far as Aberlour, turned around and disappeared out to sea. 'This has caused him to scratch his head! They have got this yellow flash on them and I do hope they turn up in the Findhorn or the Ness and somebody catches one, this would give us some idea.'

Turning from Speyside to local matters John continued 'We hope to do something similar on the Test, but there is no question at present of anyone running up and down the river with a radio tracker, but we are working on it. No doubt freezers will be emptied in advance.'

We discussed salmon open seasons on the Test and I mentioned that there had been a move to alter the season, which begins on 17 January, to the same as the trout, which opens and closes later. This would take account of the absence of the spring run, and the increase in late running fish. John: 'Over my dead body. Sitting at the bottom of the river, at Nursling, we know that virtually no fresh fish come in after the third week of August. The idea of a lengthened season at the back-end would not take account of the need to conserve stocks. Salmon start to take again in the autumn when water temperatures start to fall. If the season were extended a serious injury could be done to stocks. I would like to see the season shortened at the back-end. This ought to be done by agreement between the three major salmon fisheries, rather than by bye-laws which are terribly difficult to arrange and even more difficult to unscramble.' As to starting later, he feels that rods only catch one or two fish in February and March, they pay a heavy price for their fishing, and if they wish to go out and get themselves wet and cold in the early spring they should be allowed to do so. 'Our rods have a day away from their offices; they have a nice day out, a good lunch, rarely a fish. What is wrong with that?'

During our conversation John sat at his desk overlooking the countryside, he rocked backwards and forwards in an armchair. At any moment I expected the chair to tilt over backwards, but he seemed secure, puffing and pulling at a pipe which required frequent filling and then excavation over the wastepaper basket. At times he burst into laughter – the causes of the merriment will be found in the section on Nursling Fishery.

Two Romsey Mills

ABBEY MILL — OWNED BY DAVID STEUART
1 FEBRUARY 1989

When we arrived at Abbey Mill Fishery David was fishing for dace. He came over to talk to us of the manner in which salmon may run from below to above the mill sluices and fish pass. He is clearly dedicated to the fulfilment of the salmon's life cycle, and freedom of movement of fish in the short stretch of the river under his control.

David has an accurate mind. The first facts we must understand were these:

1. fish do not like running through dark holes and tunnels
2. no matter how large a sluice channel may be salmon enter with reluctance, or not at all, if the water pressure and speed of flow are too great.

He explained that pressure will be too great if there is a head of water of two feet from the surface to the bottom of the sluice board. If there is then another two feet from the bottom of the sluice board to the base of a fish pass a total of four feet in depth exists. This depth (with pressure being depth × density) will deter salmon regardless of the size of the opening.

He then took us to the present fish pass which had been constructed 25 years ago, and where the sluice boards may be raised and lowered by means of an iron wheel and wormed shaft. This sluice, placed in a concrete channel about 25 yards in length, could be altered to prevent fish passing up the river. It could also be operated illegally as a fish trap. No other means of journeying north existed at Abbey Mill, there being insufficient water for passage through the other seven sluices on the site.

So there it was, an obstruction under conditions of heavy water to the passage of fish. But our visit was well timed. Shortly a new Denil pass will be installed. This pass works on the basis of slowing down the flow of water by a series of baffles, and is of the same construction as that installed at Testwood and to be fitted at Nursling. David explained the complicated preparations in a letter to me dated 13 February 1989.

1. The Water Authority engineers designed the new fish pass. They get tenders from contractors who do the work. After installation they then have to get Ministry of Agriculture approval that the pass is working satisfactorily. If approved I am not allowed to interfere with it in any way that will obstruct fish passage, under severe penalties, other than for reason of maintenance (on river banks, for example, where the lowering of the river would facilitate working).
I also grant them an easement, right of way, and access across my property to inspect and maintain the fish pass.
2. The sluice which we discussed was *within* the confines of the present fish pass which was *voluntarily* constructed after pressures were placed upon the previous owners of the mill site by my friend (now dead), an adjacent riparian owner and myself, some 25 years ago, when the mill site did not have a fish pass at all. The fish could only pass the mill by swimming through sluices under the mill site (which you did not see) and via the side stream sluices, which although the fish can pass them easily by correct operation were not being operated correctly at that time, and fish were not getting upstream very easily. The fish pass made it much easier.

However, as the fish pass had within it a sluice gate, installed to allow the control of water levels upstream, it does not meet Min. of Ag. requirements, as a sluice gate that can stop the flow within a fish pass can be a very efficient fish trap if used unscrupulously, and so they would not approve it, and no attempt has been made to get approval until now as it was not an illegal structure owing to the obstruction (the mill site) having been in existance for hundreds of years. As I am concerned (along with the Southern Water Authority) that migratory fish should have completely free passage on their upstream migrations I have given them permission to redesign and improve the present fish pass to meet Min. of Ag. requirements, and although the sluice will still be within the confines of the pass, the actual pass structures will by-pass the sluice which will be completely shut down without trapping fish or affecting the flow through the pass structures. The sluice will, however, be able to be opened to allow excess water during floods to escape, and this will be the only time it will be opened other than to help get rid of water to lower upstream levels for river maintenance.

This particular sluice within the fish pass had nothing to do with the 1923 Act as the pass did not *have* to be constructed to get fish past the *obstruction*, which was the mill site, as the mill was built prior to 1873 or not altered in manner since 1873.

The Salmon & Freshwater Fisheries Act 1923 Sect. 19 states:
(1) Where since the 31st day of August 1873 in any water frequented by salmon & migratory trout –
(a) a new dam has been constructed or an existing dam has been raised or otherwise altered so as to create *increased* obstruction to the passage of salmon & migratory trout, *or any other* obstruction to the passage of salmon & migratory trout has been created, increased, or caused . . . . the owner or occupier for the time being of the dam or obstruction shall . . . . make and shall thereafter maintain in an efficient state a fish pass . . . . etc

It follows that unless evidence is available that any alterations to existing mills (dams), a mill of course contains a dam, caused *increased* obstruction to fish there is no way one can be forced to make a fish pass providing the dam existed prior to 1873 and nearly all mills have been around a very long time. Abbey Mill is mentioned in the Domesday Book.

After leaving David on that day I went upstream to an iron bridge which spans the river. Above the bridge the river divides into two. The stream coming from the left flows through a water garden, the bed of the river and the water are clear of silt and any effluent; desirable river weeds are present in abundance. Not so the stream flowing down from the right; this flow was turbid, the bed of the river covered with a brown deposit through which not a green weed showed.

ABBEY MILL – SECOND VISIT ON 26 APRIL 1989

The new Denil pass had been installed. Two sets of baffles had been set into the original channel, one at the entrance to the pass and the other yards upstream. The water rushed through at the surface of the Denil pass but moved slowly at the base. The effect was most noticeable where the channel discharged into the river and was absorbed by the main current before it reached mid-stream. Under the old system the rush reached the far bank which had been reinforced with concrete to prevent erosion.

In October I wrote to David to enquire whether the pass had proved acceptable to salmon. In the context of his reply it would be as well to record here that his salmon catch in 1988 was 14 fish:

23 October 1989

I cannot help you much, I am afraid. When the salmon were running during May and June the water was too dirty to see whether there were any salmon in the pass or not. If they did use it I didn't see any actually in the pass roll, or splash, or surface, or make their presence known. Certainly fish got up O.K. as we caught half of our meagre catch above the sluices, but they can get up through the sluices if they wish.

We caught 23 salmon, 18 of them between 8th May and 24th June – a further 5 were picked out before 11th August but they had come up in late June and were gradually caught – known fish, hard to catch,

Abbey Mill, Romsey. Baffles in a Denil fish pass.

but occasionally they would make a mistake. Three fish were still in the lies after 11th August but as they had been with us for so long we did not fish for them after that date, and not another fish came into our stretch until 19th October, when three grilse came up. The original three fish that have been with us since June are still with us, but over the last couple of days have been joined by a further eight fish – These are all upstream of the sluices but there are now also a few below the sluices since 20th October.

I saw a salmon and a trout in the Denil pass yesterday, so at least one fish has used it while I was in a position to see it. The trout may have come downstream, so may the salmon, but it is more unlikely.

At Testwood the pass is a small one and not placed to take the main run of fish – at Nursling, when I looked at the pass it was jammed solid with weed and not getting a fair chance to work, but I only saw it the once.

The new Denil pass within the confines of the old pass.

I cannot leave David without this observation: by granting permission for the Denil pass which, it is clear, could not otherwise be installed, he has sped salmon on their way.

SADDLER'S MILL

The river runs under the side of the mill where salmon may jump into the run of four small sluices to thrust their way upstream. The sluice mouths were protected in October by Bernard Aldrich with straw-filled sacks to prevent fish damaging themselves by hitting the wooden divisions between these entrances. To the left of these sluices, looking upstream from the mill pool, is the main mill race which is at a slightly higher level, and disgorges more water, than the other four. Above and around this race is a wire cage to prevent salmon leaping too high and landing on the public walkway alongside the mill. This netting also prevents poachers snatching fish.

Above the mill is a cat-walk from which salmon may be caught by spinning or by prawn or shrimp. Below, looking downstream from the mill, on the left bank is Salmon Leap house. The owner's daughter, Mrs Jane O'Brien, at one time Lord Mountbatten's groom, allowed us to take photographs from the garden. Both banks downstream of the mill belong to Broadlands, apart from a small island on the left, until Middlebridge is reached. At the southern end of the bridge are cut the words 'Rebuilt from the foundations by the County Council. 1931.'

Saddler's Mill is a tourist attraction. Many visitors arrive in the hope of seeing salmon leap, but few understand the life cycle or habits of the fish. To them the matter is mysterious. This cannot be better illustrated than by quoting from Bernard Aldrich's book of 1984, *The Ever-Rolling Stream*. 'One chap, a keen amateur photographer, repeatedly telephoned me, asking, "What time are the salmon going to jump?' I tried to explain that the fish do not work to a timetable, but he still persisted in telephoning. Eventually I became so exasperated that I just invented a time and told him the salmon would be jumping that day at 3.25 pm. This was obviously the information he required and he rang off a very satisfied man. Later that evening he phoned again in order to thank me and to marvel at the accuracy of my forecast which had enabled him to take some splendid photographs.'

Broadlands Estate

BERNARD ALDRICH — SALMON, TROUT AND COARSE
FISHERIES MANAGER
21 JUNE 1989

I_N 1956 BERNARD CAME TO BROADLANDS as under-keeper to the then head-keeper Walter Geary, whose favourite saying on salmon fishing was 'Never say never, and never say always'. Walter retired in 1964 after 51 years, Bernard took over, and is still there as curator, scholar, companion to a prince, and fisherman's advisor.

Each day, when fishing one of the salmon beats in the 1970s, I looked forward to the rattle of his Land Rover down the bank-side track or across the fields. In the back of this battered vehicle would be a long-handled gaff, a rod, his favoured, ancient Silex reel, and Jody the black labrador. Out would leap Jody whom I had given to him, to pick up a stone. She quarrelled with stones, chewing them, growling, throwing them in the air, until her teeth were worn flat. I always hoped that Bernard would take my rod to catch a fish, but he rarely fished, contenting himself, and me, by pointing out the salmon lies. He knew these places to within a foot. Every gravel patch, breakwater, pot and hole were engraved on the river map in his mind.

He taught me how to fish the upstream Mepps and Toby; how to winkle out a salmon from under the roots of a waterside oak tree with a tough little English prawn. But there are baits and there is the fly. I thought I knew about salmon fly fishing but nobody knows Broadlands fly fishing as well as he does. 'They come here from Scotland, take the water temperature, tie on a Low Water No. 10 to suit the high 60s, or even 70 degrees, and catch nothing. The Test is different. Use a No. 4.' I took his advice. He was right.

Many salmon were grassed in those years when the Broadlands catch was 300–400 fish. My diary entry of 10 August 1975 records a typical happy morning:

Beat No. 1. Lee Park. Started 10 am with a number of fish showing, and Tony rose two in Long Reach. Took 11 am 6 lb, 12 noon 7 lb and 12.30 pm 7 lb. All in the run between Kendle's Corner and Oak Tree. No. 4 Silver Doctor. Tony netted them. Had lunch and came home. Water temp. 68 deg and level low. Fish showed no interest in No. 6 Silver Doctor. After I left Frances lost a cow hooked by Long Reach on back cast. Tony lost a fish in Black Dog, and Bernard took two fish for him in Long Reach, 8 lb each on prawn.

There have been no subsequent regrets at driving home after such a morning.

When I visited Bernard in the fishing hut in June 1989 it was nostalgic to see him in the chair from which head-keepers have, historically, dispensed afternoon tea to their anglers. He produced the 1975 record book and we photographed the records for 10 August 1975. There is no secrecy at Broad-

Middlebridge (below Saddler's Mill) Romsey. Photograph by Francis Frith.

lands; the current book is always on the table for all to see. The following year, 1976, was the season of the Great Drought. Tony and myself joined forces on the river:

18 April. Rookery Beat. Under the weed net on top bridge. 11½ lb. with sea lice. First fish of the year on Broadlands shared with Tony. I found the fish, he hooked, I netted. Prawn.

The memory of that salmon is clear. I spotted him through polaroids lying under the bridge – a grey shadow. I ran back to Trees Pool where the cars were parked, fetched Tony, a prawn, and we galloped back to the salmon. The fish rose at once – to take the lead weight! He just lifted, opened his mouth, sucked in that lump of lead, spat it out and sank back to the river bed. Next time he took the prawn.

The final fish of my 1976 season is recorded in the diary as follows:

30 Sept. Lee Park. Ash Tree. Rose two fish under left bank at top of Oak Tree, second one took a prawn behind first groyne. 10 lb. A red cock fish which ran downstream and was netted by Bernard in Kendle's Corner. Tony lost a fish which weeded him in tail of Black Dog. This was the season of The Great Drought, and there was insufficient water flow to fish a fly. There were very few fish – the Broadlands total for the season was about 68, compared with 350 the previous year.

The pool, or run, known as Kendle's Corner has seen the grassing of many salmon. It is a splendid fishing place which, fittingly, records the name of G. R. Kendle, originator of Broadlands salmon fishing. Lord Mount Temple owned the estate in 1880 and G. R. Kendle was his agent. Kendle, a salmon angler, realized the potential of the undeveloped river and set about establishing a reputation for Broadlands as a salmon fishery. He caught many fish, as did his companions. The first keeper, John Cragg, was employed in 1886. Cragg took steps to improve the water under his control. Poaching, the stocking of salmon and trout, the operation of sluices, all had his attention.

In 1881 Lord Mount Temple divided the river into two sections. Until 1888 he kept the river upstream of Longbridge for his own use. Downstream, from Longbridge to the Boundary Pool, was let to Mr William Clifford who died in 1882. Mr Basil Field took over the lease and fished with Col. H. Cornwall Legh. In their first season they took 44 fish at an average weight of 10 lb; while the upper water recorded 12 fish averaging $12\frac{3}{4}$ lb.

In 1883 the lower water took 59 salmon and the upper 24. The total of 83 fish averaged $10\frac{3}{4}$ lb. The first clean salmon was taken on 17 March. In this year Col. Legh and Cragg stocked 2000 Loch Leven yearling trout and 1225 common trout (presumably brown).

1884 was a drought year. The total dropped to 35 fish but the average weight rose to $15\frac{1}{2}$ lb, presumably in spring, two or three sea-winter salmon taken before the water shortage deteriorated in the summer.

1885 – 109 salmon at an average of 13 lb.

1886 – The first salmon was taken on 24 March. Total 128 at an average of 13 lb.

1887 – A drought from April to the end of the season. First fish 26 February. Total not recorded. On 9, 10 and 11 March Col. Legh took five salmon of an average weight of $23\frac{2}{5}$ lb. Where are such fish today?

1888 – The upper water 20 fish averaging $14\frac{1}{2}$ lb; the lower 31 fish averaging 15 lb. The original lease to William Clifford having expired, the lower fishing was let to five rods at £70 each on a yearly tenancy. At the same time Lord Mount Temple was able to let the fishing from six fields in the Parish of Romsey to Samuel Turner Blake for the term of 14 years at the annual rent of £20.

The trout stocking of five years earlier now bore fruit. On 12 May Mr T. Jenvey of Romsey caught a trout of $10\frac{1}{2}$ lb on a shrimp in Middle Bridge Pool. On 14 May Mr Kendle took another of 9 lb in the same manner and place. Fat trout have been caught there over the years. C. Ernest Pain wrote in 1934 that he had killed a trout below Romsey of 3 lb 14 oz which was 'only eighteen inches and a quarter long'. The presence of a butcher and slaughterhouse adjacent to Middlesbridge may have had something to do with the matter!

1889 – The rent to six rods rose to £80 each. Mr Kendle was clearly doing his financial duty by the estate as well as carrying out his practical responsibilities on the river. The rods received good value. On 14 June The Hon. Alan Charteris 'had a splendid fish of 38 lb on a Butcher out of The Cowman's Hole'. At the end of the season Col. French took 13 salmon in three days. The total take was 103 fish at an average of $12\frac{1}{3}$ lb.

1890 – Very dry. The heaviest fish of 29 lb taken by Mr A. Smith on a 'Childers' from the Boundary Pool. Two tagged fish marked T No. 1 and T No. 2 were caught but returned. The origin of the tags, which were in the dorsal fin, is not known.

1891 – Very dry. Attention turns to trout as well as salmon. Three rods caught 21 trout weighing $68\frac{1}{4}$ lb. The salmon catch held up at 114 fish.

1892 – A fair supply of water all through the season. The first fish on 25 February, and the heaviest of 30 lb, taken from Cottage Pool on a Butcher – both by Col. French who seems to have been both skilled and persistent. There is the first mention of a lady – 'Mrs H. Birkbeck took 8 trout weighing 29 lb'. On 2 September Capt. Streatfield killed a trout of $11\frac{1}{2}$ lb 'which up to this date is the largest ever got in the water'. The salmon totalled 130.

1893 – Dry. A fish of 32 lb from Needle Pool. Total 37 salmon. Complaints on water extraction by farmers for irrigation. Cragg reports on flooding of water meadows through the hatches and the consequent stranding and demise of young salmon when the water meadows were drained. He suggests the installation of gratings. His concern mounts about netsmen at sea and poaching on the spawning beds. He makes a request for watchers 'and it requires two men hear [sic] at Romsey by night to look after the salmon during the time they are spawning on the beds. And one man by day'.

1894 – There is mention of weed cutting in May, July and September. Total 65 salmon.

1895 – Cragg's pleas bear fruit. £75 was paid to two farmers for shutting down their hatches to the water meadows for three days each week. Capt. The Hon. Victor Montagu takes a 26 lb salmon. Total 87 fish.

1896 – 64 fish. Col. Grant one of 29 lb in Long Reach.

1897 – The trout record breaker! $13\frac{1}{4}$ lb to Mr W. Ashley. Mr Warrender a close second with $12\frac{1}{2}$ lb – both in May.

Total salmon 46.

SALMON IN BERNARD'S TIME

Bernard and I talked of the days when I had fished this water, the good years when salmon seethed on the five salmon beats: Rookery, Lee Park, Longbridge, Moorcourt and Grove. They run from just below Broadlands

House to the southern extremity at Boundary Pool on Grove. Those were the days. Plenty of salmon and the water as clear as in Augustus Grimble's day at the beginning of the 20th century, when he wrote 'In the shallows the water looks as clear as drinking water in a tumbler when held up to the light.'

From our conversation on the reducing salmon runs, and numbers of spawning fish, it became clear that one of Bernard's main worries was the reduction of both water flows and purity. I asked whether the salmon stocking programme could become self-perpetuating after a short-term boost of introduced smolts. He hoped so but was grievously worried about the state of the river. Many gravel areas, formerly sites of spawning redds, now become covered with silt due to reduced water flows: 'The Test is now a settling river rather than a flushing river.' In the old days they cut all the weed at the end of the season; high water was then expected virtually throughout the winter. All silt and rubbish was flushed from the bed. The water would clear by March and remain at a good height. Today it may not clear until June. Another factor is the ever increasing amount of phosphates and nitrates in the river. These washings are the consequence of intensive farming to the river edge in areas previously covered by water meadows. Not only fertilizers, silt as well is carried down the ditches to the river. Blanket weed, starwort and bulrushes now take up station in the reduced, polluted flow. The Broadlands section of the river suffers from a growing quantity of treated effluent from the expanded Romsey sewage works. A diffuser has been installed below Middlebridge; this 28-inch pipe is right in the middle of the river. Nobody knows how much effluent is discharged other than those operating the system. Blanket weed flourishes below the opening. It is mind-jolting to know that this is taking place on the old Game Fair site above Broadlands House.

These problems of pollution and flow reduction have reduced salmon spawning on the estate. Bernard drew my attention to the fact that in the 1880s, when salmon were not encouraged above Romsey, they spawned on the estate. In the 1950s they were active in considerable numbers on Rookery Beat, 50 or 60 pairs. Redds were cut by the fishing hut, and in all the side streams. Today few pairs spawn on Broadlands. The increase in large stocked trout reduces the survival of fry and alevins. How often have large trout disgorged little fish? Some of these fry are salmon.

On the positive side the danger to salmon is recognized, steps are being taken; helping hands extended. First among these are Alan Mann's smolts (page 121). Whether this will provide a permanent increase in the population may depend on whether salmon offspring will survive in the deteriorating river conditions.

At least we shall learn much about their survival through the salmon-tagging scheme and the newly installed fish counters. Bernard described the identification system. When smolts are to be released to migrate down-river to the sea, the Ministry of Agriculture sends a team to Alan Mann's hatchery at King's Somborne. They inject micro-tags into the foreheads of the smolts. The tag is a hair-thin piece of wire $\frac{1}{8}$ inch long which records the date and place of release, and the size of the smolt. The adipose fin is then clipped for immediate recognition. Subsequently, after the marine stage, if a rod catches a salmon with a clipped adipose, Bernard has to say 'I'm sorry, but I'm going to cut off its head'. The head is then collected

Bernard Aldrich in the Broadlands fishing hut.

by Southern Water, a scanner collects the hidden tag and the history of the fish is revealed.

Then there are the new fish passes installed in 1988 and 1989 at Romsey, Nursling and Testwood. These will be a help 'if they work'. He has not seen the pass at Nursling, but a visit to Testwood did not give rise to optimism. He considers this pass is too far up Testwood Pool, has too little water and is beyond the main sluices where fish will tend to congregate. This view is in line with the information given to me by Steve Westwell, the Testwood keeper, who confirmed that salmon do not favour the new pass. Time will tell, but all on the river are on the salmon's side.

The timing of salmon runs into the river has altered over the years. The large spring salmon of Kendle's day are gone but, one hopes, not for ever. Grilse now predominate and their time is from July onwards. Bernard would like to see the salmon season altered, if the runs increase, to take account of the later arrival of the fish. He suggests that trout and salmon have the same season: 3 April to the end of October, instead of starting for salmon in February and ending on 2 October. In that month, in 1988, when there were many fish passing on their way upstream, he constructed a new breakwater. Within 10 minutes there was a fish showing alongside.

TROUT AT BROADLANDS

The Broadlands fishery is commercial, as is now the case on almost the whole length of the river. The fishing has to show a profit. Salmon runs were, and are, reducing. Trout must fill the gap.

Up to seven years ago there were six salmon beats, the Lord Louis Beat, being the bank opposite to Rookery Beat, having been added to the original five. These comprised the whole of the Broadlands main river downstream of Broadlands House.

As the demand for salmon fell, along with the catches, Bernard stocked the three lower beats with brown trout, which were fished for until the end of June. As grilse arrived in July the beats then reverted to salmon for the remainder of the season at a reduced rent. The demand for trout rods was phenomenal and for salmon rods disheartening. To satisfy the demand the lower beats became trout only after three years.

Bernard has increased his trout rearing capacity beyond the present need. If salmon continue to decline he would also convert the upper three beats to trout. The river is wide on the estate with no check to trout movement. Brownies only are stocked because 'the browns hold station better in the river than rainbow trout'. Fly life is present in abundance: iron blue, blue-winged olive, mayfly, sedges, hawthorn. 'You name it. We've got it. They are all here.'

Running down from the estate hatchery is the trout stream created in 1964. This is narrow and deep in places. In this protected water rainbows are stocked, and provided the first trout fishing under Bernard's care.

THE COARSE FISHERIES

The first coarse fishery came into being through the extraction of gravel on the lower estate for the construction of the M27 motorway. Bernard suggested to Lord Mountbatten that instead of in-filling the gravel pit it be converted to a coarse fishery. His Lordship agreed. The contractors, instead of re-filling the pit, built an island, fenced the area and planted trees. 'The lake has turned into a very good coarse fishery. Pike, carp, perch, tench, trout, roach. Everything that swims.'

Many people fish, up to 150 or 200 at a time, and daily, season and club tickets are available. Competitions are held. A second lake has now been opened at Longbridge. To help cope with these fishing enterprises Bernard has two under-keepers: one on the river and the other at the coarse fisheries.

THE PRAWN

When I first fished at Broadlands my knowledge of the prawn was, to put it mildly, sketchy. 'Let the prawn dolly about close to the river bed, sway in the current, feel the line in your fingers for nibbling salmon.' Many morsels of advice came my way. One morning I arrived at Bernard's hut and there, crouched by the fence post closest to the river, was an angler. He was tweedy, well weathered and red of neck, a colour which might have cost a lot of money and brought profit to the Spey valley. I watched him from behind, hoping to emulate his concentrated attention. Nothing distracted him, his fingers trembled on the twitching line as he stared into the water, steadying himself against the post. I didn't like to ask his advice, to break the concentration of this expert, and so drove off to my beat.

At tea time I returned. He hadn't moved. 'Has he had one?' I asked. 'Not likely', was Bernard's comment 'but he has had two bottles of Scotch.'

Nursling

EARLY DAYS

Nursling will be seen within the *Redbridge Hundred* in John Speed's *Hantshire* (circa 1610). The Nursling Mills are described in History of Hampshire and Isle of Wight Vol. 3.

> From early times a water-mill was appurtenant to the manor of Nursling Beaufo, being mentioned as early as 1255. It is probable also that there was another mill in the parish appurtenant to the manor of Nursling Prior, for one is included in the extent of 'Notesselinge' in the *Domesday Book*. In the Chancery decree of 1619 two water corn-mills and three 'fullingstocke' thereunto adjoining called Nursling Mills are mentioned as having been leased to Andrew Mundy by Sir Richard Mill. One of them seems to have fallen into disuse by the beginning of the eighteenth century, and there is now only one water-mill in the parish. A several fishery in the River Test was appurtenant to the manor of Nursling Prior. The prior sometimes had some difficulty in maintaining his rights. Thus in 1387 he brought an action against John Goldsmith of Southampton, William Fisher, Robert Goudyer, and Richard Lobbe for fishing in his fishery at Nursling and carrying off 200 lampreys, 300 salmon, 200 trout, 4000 eels, and other fish to the value of £40. John Goldsmith, who was at this time holding the manor of Testwood on a nine years' lease from Sir Thomas West, asserted that the fishery in the Test between 'Asshedych' on the north and 'Dodepole' on the south was common to the lords of the manors of Nursling Prior and Testwood, and that therefore he and his servants were justified in fishing therein. The case was therefore adjourned for further evidence, but with what result does not appear.

The Mill family connection, noted above in 1619, was again recorded in

1728 when the present mill was built, on the wall of which is a stone plaque engraved:

'This building stands on a frame of large beech timber which was given by Sir Richard Mill, Bart. in memory of whose kindness this stone was placed here by

H. K. 1728'

I have been unable to discover the identity of 'H.K.'. Today the fishery is owned by the Barker-Mills Estate.

When I met John Potter on 5 July 1989 he told me that his grandfather had had some form of a lease, with others, since 1915. When he died, John's father took over and on his death John succeeded. 'It hasn't become any cheaper over the years.'

The major part of my interview with John Potter concerned the salmon rehabilitation programme (page 154), but we also discussed subjects relevant to Nursling. John said:

'We use fly, minnow and prawn. Over the years something has changed. We always used to fish the fly. I personally fish the fly almost every Saturday throughout the year. I don't say I do any worse than I did, but last year I only caught one. I don't know why. Vic [the keeper] doesn't know why, but there are nagging doubts that there are less fish about than previously. Anyway, they don't seem to like to take the fly. We also use minnow and prawn. Recently at Nursling the worm has been creeping in. In order to be seen to be doing something to conserve fish stocks, particularly at the back-end when the worm is at its most effective, the three fisheries [Nursling, Testwood and Broadlands] got together this spring of 1989. They decided that Nursling and Testwood would ban the worm as from that day. Broadlands would also phase it out as soon as they could. This won't save an awful lot of fish, but it will bring notice to the rods that they have to do their bit.'

John recalled a few incidents from over the years:

'One morning in February my brother and Vic were digging a flight pond for duck. Two lords were fishing, corpulent men, leaning forward with rod butts stuck in their tummies. My brother said, "Doesn't that give you heart-ache, Vic?" He replied "No Sir, but it gives them back-ache. They'll be gone by half-past two." They were.

'Leonard Court [the keeper] was Vic's uncle from whom Vic took over. Leonard lived until he was 92 years old. The first fish I ever rose on fly I failed to hook. Leonard was with me. He took me by the shoulders, looked me in the eye and said "Don't you ever let me see you do that again." I had seen the fish come and pulled the fly away. I don't think I have knowingly repeated that mistake. He did much the same to my brother Nigel. He couldn't say Nigel. He said "Master Nidal. If you do that again I'll throw you in the river".

'Once in the winter it was snowing horizontal. Leonard was all huddled up under a bush and we were pushing the ice out of the rod rings. He came up to us and said "You know I'm paid to do this. You do it for fun".'

This reminded me of the incident during a hard winter at Nursling recorded by Pain in his book on the Test.

'The next water downstream is Nursling. Here after a prolonged frost a quantity of ground ice had once formed in the bed of the Little River, and when the thaw came there was a high tide which left huge blocks of ice in the meadow. In one block was a salmon looking like a stuffed fish.'

Nursling Salmon Fishery

VIC FOOT — SALMON-KEEPER
6 JULY 1989

THERE HAVE BEEN THREE HEAD-KEEPERS: Albert Johnson who took up his duties in 1890; Leonard Court (uncle of Vic Foot) succeeded him in 1901 and Vic Foot. When Vic was $13\frac{1}{2}$ years old there was a vacancy at Nursling. The school leaving age was then 14 years and so he could not be accepted. Another man was taken on but left within the year to join the merchant navy. After leaving school Vic delivered newspapers but, when the vacancy arose for the second time 'I was down there at once. Haven't looked back since. Best thing that ever happened to me. Apart from my National Service years, commencing in 1945, I've been here ever since, and that'll be 47 years this August.' After the army, in which he served in Germany and emerged a full corporal, acting sergeant, he returned to Nursling and looked about for a wife. Down the road was an old farmer, living with his niece, whom all at Nursling now call Won. 'I used to go and fish the old pond in front of the farm more regular than I should do. I called it Mermaid's Hole.' They were married in 1953. In the fullness of time Vic succeeded Leonard Court, and there he still is, as happy as a sand boy.

I met Vic on Thursday afternoon as he was taking a student in his car to cut weed with a pole scythe in the Little River. I joined them. Rods had been fishing that morning, but the tide had come in and fishing would not recommence until later in the evening. We talked as we walked along the bank. Vic looked at the river – 'At one time we had a load of escaped rainbow trout here from the trout farm; hundreds of them. We caught as many as we could on bread paste and other baits to free the river, but some set sail for the sea. They came back three or four months later, half a pound heavier, covered with sea lice. They were absolutely beautiful to eat. The colour of the flesh was perfect; as good as sea trout. Some were gobbled-up at sea, but their instinct made the survivors return. One year we had one of 7½ lb, a short little thing, as fat as butter, the flesh as red as anything. When I came here first we cut the weeds middle of May. That was alright until the June cut and then August. Now we have dirty water and you've got to cut the damn things every two weeks, particularly with this warm water. Last year every three weeks. I blame nitrates and the ammonia from fish farms.'

We returned to the house in front of which is a wire link fence in place of the wooden palings on which salmon were hung for photographs in earlier years. On the right of the fishing cottage is a wooden addition decorated with fearsome pikes' heads. Inside we were greeted by Won who made a pot of tea. 'In the beginning of the year, when fish are scarce, he'll come in and give a little twitch, a tug, to my sleeve. He means he had a nibble or a pull from a salmon. Just a touch.'

Over tea Vic reminisced, photographs were examined of historical catches, the pages of past fishing records leafed and studied.

'If you could see the expressions on the faces of some of the old gentlemen when they get their first fish. They are hooked for evermore. Their object is then to get another. I remember one gentleman I went with years ago. He lost a fish and kept on about it. I said "All I can say is, I hope you lose a lot more." He said "That's not a very nice thing to say", but I replied "If by chance you don't lose any more fish you will not do much more fishing.' He said "If you want to look at it that way, I suppose you're right." If you knew when you went out you were going to hook a fish, and you knew you were going to land it, you might as well go to MacFisheries and buy one.

'At one time we had a number of trout fishermen who had not yet caught a salmon. One of these was very good at trout. His first fish came up – he pulled the fly away, same with the second. He then said "If I do it again, push me in." Lo and behold, a third salmon came up and he tweaked his rod. He just couldn't stop the reaction. I didn't push him in, but he became a very good salmon fisherman and tied his own flies.

'Look at this photograph of Sir Thomas and Lady Sopwith with 21 salmon. They caught 19 and then came in for tea. Old Sir Thomas said "We're going to have another half-hour to make it 20." I said "Alright,

Nursling Salmon Fishery, 24 May 1954. Sir Thomas and Lady Sopwith. 21 salmon.

Sir." I went down with her ladyship and Sir Thomas went below a
bridge. She had a try, but without result. I sat on the seat looking at
her, and picked up the old fly rod with a Hairy Mary on. I flicked it
over the top and pulled off a bit of line and "bang", there he was. That
was the twentieth. I happened to look across on the main river and there
was old Sir Thomas with Ted, his keeper. Sir T's rod was doubled up,
and they had the 21st. Ted was Cecil Hill's father who built the little
hatchery at Wherwell.

'One day in February the water was a bit dirty. Lady Sopwith
telephoned in the morning to enquire about conditions. I said it was
not much good. She said "We'll send down Ted." Sends old Ted down
and we had a cup of tea. Ted goes out, hooks a fish in the first
breakwater and had a stroke. Down he went and died that evening. The
fish got off. I had virus pneumonia at that time and couldn't go out.
When Won went to him and picked up the rod the fish had gone.

'Sir Thomas Sopwith and Sir Richard Fairey used to share and
interchange their fishing days. Sir Richard's son, Dick, lost both legs
during the war. He ferried aeroplanes from America to England. They
went out by boat and then flew the 'planes back. He lost his legs when
the ship taking them out was torpedoed. Dick used to stump about on
his artificial legs and fly over Nursling very low to land at Eastleigh
airport. After a little while he would arrive from the airport in a taxi.
He then did his fishing. Later the taxi would collect him to take him
back to the airport. On the way home he would again fly over the river.

Nursling Salmon Fishery. 43lb salmon caught by J. Wilson Potter, 13 March 1918.

One time he came by so low that the trees shook. I told him about it the next week. I said "You were a bit close to them trees, Mr Richard, weren't you." "Ah", he said, "I'd probably had a whisky too much".

'In about 1967, when the motorway was being completed, they straightened the river for the bridge construction. They had a couple of drag lines working and the river came down very dirty. That was on a Sunday from 9 am to 9 pm. The next day it was slightly tinged, and on that Monday night it poured with rain and the river became very dirty again. On the Tuesday the Rod Box had half the water and the conditions were perfect. The place was filled with fish after all the dirt had gone down. They came up from the estuary on the flood. The Rod Box came and caught 21 fish of about 5 lb or 6 lb each. It was a grilse run in the summer.'

Nursling Mill. Commemorative stone to Sir Richard Mill, Bart, 1728.

Vic pulled out a photograph of John Potter taken on 28 April 1950 with two salmon of 26 lb and 37½ lb. 'He was carrying a little less weight than today. Since then he has sampled the good life. We all put on a bit as the years go by.' He looked at me. 'You're alright. Been living the life of a puritan, I expect.'

One diary entry read: '2 fish for farmers'. Vic explained:

'It used to be the practice years ago to give half a salmon at Easter to the five farmers on the banks. Today we are lucky to get one salmon by mid-April. About two years ago we had one by 21 April. This year it has been a trifle better: one in January and one in February. About 1962 or 1963, on 17 January, we had 7 or 8 fish of which I took three. On that day I was on one side of the river with a fish on and Sir Thomas was on the other side, also with a fish. He was going upstream with his and I was going down with mine. We passed each other and he shouted "That was a bit of luck, wasn't it." We had about 13 fish that week and went on and caught a lot after that.'

Questioned about fishing tackle he told me of the following incidents:

'Years ago we used gut. Nylon wasn't about. This gut was already attached to plugs and prawns and minnows and these tackles were soaked in a side stream ready for use. You had to keep gut damp. Fly lines, and casts with flies were also streamed out. There might be six or eight rods in position keeping the tackle wet. One day a gentleman tossed in a prawn on his rod and went in to lunch. When we came out we found an eel had taken the prawn and twisted up all the tackle. On another occasion a fisherman came down with a sink-and-draw tackle consisting of two trebles and a pin to push into the prawn. The trebles were bound to the tackle with red silk and the pin was painted red. He tossed this into the top of the Drawing Room Pool just to soak, there was no prawn mounted, and went in to lunch. When we came out we saw that the line had run out. We landed that salmon, which must have been attracted by the red tackle.'

Vic greatly approves of the salmon rehabilitation scheme and Alan

Mann's efforts at his hatchery. Information on salmon numbers and movements is gathered at Nursling by electronic equipment. We walked up the Little River to a small building housing a fish counter and water flow meter. Above this hut are three hatches which salmon are unable to pass due to an electric beam which imparts a shock. Instead they swim through an underwater tube, which houses the counter, to the river above.

We then drove to Nursling Mill on the Main River to be met by two Alsatian dogs. 'Don't worry. They only bite Southern Water employees as they taste sweeter and have fingers like sausages.' The Mill ceased to work in 1957.

There are fish passes, and counters with synchronized flash cameras installed below the Nursling Mill Pool. Not only are salmon counted, but

Nursling. Vic Foot, head keeper. By 1990 he had worked at the salmon fishery for 48 years. Pike heads surround the doorway.

a photograph is taken of those long enough to activate the mechanism by passing over three sensitive lines in the bed of the pass.

Driving back to the house I heard about poaching which was a considerable problem between 1962 and the late 1970s. Lord Mountbatten instituted a salmon squad of a sergeant and four constables. In one week 22 poachers were caught and Vic recovered 19 salmon, some of which were shown in court. Many convictions resulted. This squad was known as 'Lord Mountbatten's heavies'.

On leaving Vic and Won I was allowed to take with me a selection of fishing diaries; these I had photocopied, and then returned a fortnight later. The following are some extracts:

In 1917 rods fished between March and June, when it appears the season closed, apart from three fish taken on 4, 13 and 20 August by F. Dixon. These salmon weighed 20, 6 and 19 lb. The dates of each catch are given, the weight of the salmon and whether taken on fly, prawn or minnow. The summary for the season is as follows:

1917	
R.B.P.	1
Cookson	1
Potter	11
Mackinnon	6
F. Dixon	28
Currie	6
F. Dixon's friends	13
Johnson & farmers	4
H. Dixon	16
Appleford	1
	—
	87

The average weight of these fish was a trifle over 16 lb. 24 were sent to London and other destinations. The cost of fish baskets, rod boxes and telegrams to advise of dispatch were recorded laboriously in ink blotched copper-plate writing in a cash book.

	£	s	d
March telegram			9
1 rod box – D		1	
1 fish to London – P		1	3
1 fish to Winchester – P			6
1 fish to London – D		1	2
1 fish to London P		1	9
1 fish to London D		1	4
2 fish to London P		2	7
1 fish to Wellington P		1	3
1 fish to London P		1	3
Telegram P			9
1 rod P			4
1 telegram			$10\frac{1}{2}$
2 baskets of fish P		2	
1 Wire for Mr Potter			9
2 fish for Mr Potter		2	7
1 fish for Mr Potter		1	5
2 fish for Mr Potter		3	1

May	£	s	d
1 fish for Mr Dixon		1	4
2 fish for Mr Potter		1	2
1 fish for Mr Potter		1	5
1 fish for Mr Potter		1	4
1 fish for Mr Dixon			6
1 fish for Mr Potter		1	
1 fish for Mr Potter		1	
1 fish for Mr Bird		1	
1 Wire for Mr Bird			10
1 fish for Mr Potter		1	1

There is also the disturbing cost of 'brakwater'   1   0   0

(Little River)   Sea. Trout. 1952.   Weight lbs

Date	Name		Weight		
May. 19.	Dr. Exner.	L R	4. lbs	4	
June. 11.	Mr Chivers	L R	5. lbs	5	
June. 20.	Mr Potter	L R	4. 8. lbs	4. 8	
June. 23.	Mr Sopwith.	L R	7. lbs	7	
June. 26.	Mr Penny	L R	8. lbs	8	
June. 28.	Mr Potter	L R	5.4. lbs	5. 4.	
July. 1.	Mr Sopwith.	L R	5. lbs	5	
July. 3.	Cmd Holbrook.	L R	7. 5. lbs	7. 5	
July. 4.	Mr Potter.	L R	5.4. lbs	5. 4	
July. 7.	Mr Sopwith.	L R	6. lbs	6	
July 8.	Mrs Sopwith.	L R	6 lbs	6	
July 9.	Mr Thompson 3. Mr Chivers 2		5. 4 4. 3. 2. lbs	5. 4 4. 3. 2.	
July 10.	Mr Penny	L R	9. 4. lbs		
July 11.	Mr Potter	L R	5. 4. lbs		
July 12.	Mr. J. Baker	L R	4. . lbs		
July 14.	Mr. Sopwith	L R	6. 5. lbs		
July 15	Dr. Morgan	L R	4. lbs		
July 16	Mr Chivers	L R	6. 5.		
July 19	Mr Potter	L R	2. 2 .2 .2 .2. 2. 2. 2. lbs	(38)	
July 21	Sir. R. Fairey	L R	7. 2.		
July 22.	Mr. Ward.	L R	4. 3. 3.		
July 23	Mr Chivers.	L R	4.		
July 24	Mr. Penny.	L R	5. 4.		
July 26	Mr. Potter	L R	3. 2. 2. 2. 2. 1½.		
July 28	Sir. R. Fairey	L R	3. 2.		
Aug 1 + 2.	Mr Potter + Sons	L R	5. 4. 3. 3.	58	

Nursling. The Little River. Sea trout records.

In 1919 a greater variety of rods fished and the catch rose to 102 salmon at an average weight of $15\frac{1}{2}$ lb. The fishing took place between February 11 and July 15. If rods fished thereafter it is not recorded. Of these fish the prawn accounted for 49, the fly took 46, a spoon 1, and the minnow 2. The baits for 4 fish being obscured.

Diaries for many years were available. Space does not permit their inclusion, but the following record of sea trout caught in 1952 in the Little River indicates Nursling's potential.

			lb
May	19	Dr Exner	4
June	11	Mr Chivers	5
	20	Mr Potter	4 & 8
	23	Mr Sopwith	7
	26	Mr Penny	8
	28	Mr Potter	5 & 4
July	1	Mr Sopwith	5
	3	Cmd. Holbrook	7 & 5
	4	Mr Potter	5 & 4
	7	Mr Sopwith	6
	8	Mrs Sopwith	6
	9	Mr Thompson	5, 4 & 4
		Mr Chivers	3 & 2
	10	Mr Penny	9 & 4
	11	Mr Potter	5 & 4
	12	Mr J. Baker	4
	14	Mr Sopwith	6 & 5
	15	Dr Morgan	4
	16	Mr Chivers	6 & 5
July	19	Mr Potter	8 of 2 lb each
	21	Sir R. Fairey	7 & 2
	22	Mr Ward	4, 3 & 3
	23	Mr Chivers	4
	24	Mr Penny	5 & 4
	26	Mr Potter	3, 2, 2, 2, 2, $1\frac{1}{2}$
	28	Sir R. Fairey	3 & 2

Aug 1 & 2 Mr Potter & Sons   5, 4, 3, 3.
         5   Mr Ward & Mr Chivers   5, 4, 2, 2.
         6   Mr Chivers   4 & 3
         7   Mr Penny   5, 3 & 3
         8   Mr Potter & Sons   13 & 4
         9   Mr Potter & Sons   4 & 3
       11   Sir R. Fairey   4
       12   Mr Ward & Mr Chivers   4 & 3
       13   Mr Chivers   4, 3, 3, 2.
       14   Mr Penny   5 & 4
       15   Mr Potter & Sons   3 & 2
       16   J. Potter   4, 3 & 2
       19   Mr Ward & Mr Chivers   6, 4, 4, 2.
       20   Mr Chivers   4
       22   Mr Potter   4, 2, 2.
       23   Mr J. Potter   5 & 3
       26   Mr Ward & Mr Chivers   5, 4, 2, 2.
       27   Mr Chivers & friends   not recorded

DATE	WHERE CAUGHT	RIVER	No. of RODS	FLY or no. caught	FISH	WEIGHT Lbs. Ozs.	TOTAL	REMARKS	DATE
28th	HR2	Fly		2	14.5 lls		19	Maj Ashly Cooper	
29th	HR3 R1	Fly		R	16, 14, 9, 5, lls		44	Maj A Cooper Maj Allan Mr Chivers	

Nursling. Main River. John Ashley-Cooper preferred the fly.

188

There follow diary entries notable either for the catch or the identity of the rods, or both.

1954 May 24 Fly 3, minnow 10, prawn 8. 21 fish. 15, 14, 14, 14, 14, 12, 12, 12, 15, 13, 13, 13, 10, 10, 10, 10, 10, 10, 10, 9, 9. lb. Sir Thomas & Lady Sopwith Little River 19, Main River 2

1954 June 1 Fly 3, prawn 7. 10 fish. 17, 13, 13, 13, 12, 12, 9, 9, 9, 8 lb. Sir R. Fairey & Sir John Slessor. Little River 7, Main River 3.

1954 June 23 Fly 4, prawn 2. 6 fish. 15, 14, 12, 10, 6, 5 lb. Mr Potter, Maj. Ashley-Cooper Little River 2, Main River 4

1954 was the season when salmon catches peaked:

January	7
February	8
March	65
April	119
May	232
June	202
July	132
August	56
September	37
	———
	858

Total weight of salmon 10,079 lb.
Average 11$\frac{3}{4}$ lb.
Total sea trout 45 at an average of just over 2 lb.

1956 May 19 Fly, prawn and minnow. 9 fish. 12, 12, 12, 8, 9, 10, 10, 11, 12 lb Mr Potter, Lord Louis Mountbatten, Lord Portal, Mr Wilson. Little River 7, main River 2.

1957 March 19 Plug. 2 fish. 18, 14 lb. Mr R. Fairey & Lord Brabazon. Little River 1, Main River 1.

Testwood Salmon Fishery. The upper waters above the hatches and the new salmon pass.

Testwood

STEVE WESTWELL — SALMON-KEEPER
2 FEBRUARY 1989

I VISITED STEVE AT Testwood Fishing Lodge where he is resident water-keeper in charge of Testwood Pool, the lower water below the bridge to the lodge, and the upper beat above the sluices and the new salmon pass.

The river from Old Redbridge, at Totton, up through the marshes to Testwood and Testwood Pool belongs to the Barker-Mills estate. The river divides above Redbridge: the main river runs up to Testwood; the little river to Nursling Fishery with the Drawing Room pool. Testwood Pool is at the tidal limit of the main river. The two rivers rejoin above Nursling Mill and Conagar Bridge. From this upper junction the river runs north through Broadlands to Romsey.

Steve came to the river from Lancashire in 1976, the year of the great drought, and spent some time at Nursling before taking up his present position. In that dry summer many grilse ran into the pool, but the water was so warm that 'the poor things were lying about gasping'. His comment made me search my fishing diary for my own experiences of that hot season. The record listed six salmon and grilse to my rod at Broadlands in 1976 out of a total for the estate of 68 fish. In 1975 I grassed 10 salmon out of a total of 350. Steve indeed arrived when the river was in a hot and sorry state.

He recounted that the peak of salmon fishing on the Test was in the 1950s. It was said that, for each yard of bank, more salmon were caught at Testwood and Nursling, and possibly Broadlands, than on the prime beats of the Tay. Today about 75% of salmon caught are grilse weighing between 5 lb and 6 lb with a top weight of 8 lb. Grilse enter the river from July until the end of the season. The remaining 25% are two-sea-winter fish, of which only a few enter in April, May and June. If one went back to the 1860s and 1870s, from then until about 1960, two-sea-winter salmon made up the major portion of the run. These fish entered between the beginning of April and the end of June at weights between 10 lb and 15 lb, with a few heavier fish.

He considers that the length of time salmon spend at sea tends to go in cycles. Today we are in a grilse era and this, as in the past, may be succeeded by a predominance of two-sea-winter fish.

The salmon catch for Testwood in 1988 was 327 fish. Steve considers that anything over 300 is good. Of these 40% were caught on the top beat, above the sluices, and 60% in the pool. In the summer of that year there were only two really wet months: July and October. On one wet July day grilse were following each other head to tail under Testwood bridge watched by Steve and Brian Parker of Bossington, near Stockbridge. 'The story went about that the Bossington keeper had seen a tremendous run of grilse – but they didn't finish off the account and say that the Bossington keeper was standing on Testwood bridge at the time.'

Sadly, the sea trout run has reduced. They peaked in the years 1978 to 1980. There was a good catch in 1981 but the run halved in the following season. There is today 'a rare old mix' of sizes: some of 12 oz, many weigh between 2 lb and 3 lb. In 1988 the largest caught pulled down the scales to $11\frac{1}{2}$ lb. That fish was caught in the pool just off the eel racks. Two years earlier a sea trout of $13\frac{1}{2}$ lb was taken. The record for Testwood stands at $20\frac{1}{2}$ lb which is a very large specimen for any river. For sea trout fishing at night Steve favours Stoat's Tails and silver bodied tubes. 'Anything with a bit of black in it. You can chuck in what you like when they're really on the go. Some favour a dark fly with a flashy body – black and silver with a speck of red.' 'Size of fly?' I asked. 'Well, you can try a 2 in or 3 in long elver type, but the standard length is about 1 in. Not many people fish small traditionals: Peter Ross, Grouse and Claret, that sort of thing. But, they will tie those on as a dropper. There's nothing like a dropper if the sea trout are a bit down. Skate a bob across the surface – they explode upwards from the deeps.' His sea trout fishing is exciting, but is secondary to salmon. The rods are let for salmon for the season, and they can go on and fish at night if feeling so inclined.

We walked over the eel traps to the sluices. There a bank was being repaired with oak boards tied in with steel wires. Beyond the sluices a new fish pass, with a depth of 3 feet, had been constructed under the direction of the Southern Water Authority. This pass had been built to ensure a free run for salmon to the upper river. Fish can still make their migration to the higher river via the old sluices, and many seemed to prefer the old route. Beyond the sluices and the new fish pass is the upper river. There the water may rise in heavy spate down both the Test and Blackwater which runs in on the west bank. Recently Southern Water put in automatic flood relief hatches, operated by sensors monitoring the upstream level. Prior to these automatic arrangements Steve had to get up in the night to open the hatches in heavy weather. He still does! Waking at first light on the first flood after the installation of the new devices he found the fields awash. Water was everywhere, and the fishing hut in danger. The electrical connections to the sensors had been made incorrectly. As the water rose the hatches closed. He uses the electric motors to raise and lower the hatches but prefers to press buttons by hand rather than rely on invisible eyes.

And the tide? This brings in fish, particularly when the flood at springs raises the level by 4 feet in the pool. Sometimes the fishing hut is almost awash.

After passing the eel traps, the sluices, new fish pass and the flood relief hatches, we continued down the east side of the pool to the iron bridge. There, at the run-off of the pool, Steve had increased the depth from 4 feet to 9 feet of water by dredging out almost 1000 tons of silt. The increased depth would give cover to salmon which, in the past, had been frightened by walkers hanging their heads over the bridge. This dredging revealed a stone ridge below the bridge – a sure future lie for salmon by day and sea trout by night. Downstream from the bridge is the lower beat. This water is no longer fished separately. Today it is covered at times by rods fishing the pool, but few fish are caught. One or two may be taken under the right bank, but not in the main run.

Trout are not a major feature, although the rods sometimes spend an hour or two on the upper river at mayfly time if salmon fishing is quiet. Poachers are seldom a problem. This is understandable. Steve is large and formidable and so are his dogs!

On leaving I felt that much is being done along the river to assist the upstream passage of salmon. The new fish pass, the one at Nursling, the pass in Romsey at Abbey Mill, the efforts of Bernard Aldrich and Alan Mann are co-ordinated by Robin Crawshaw of Southern Water. A comprehensive effort is being made. It remains to be seen whether the spawning environment is still suitable for continuous natural regeneration.

Old Redbridge. The mouth of the river Test at Southampton Water.

Epilogue

F<small>ROM TIME TO TIME</small> in recent years I have fulfilled requests to value the
fishing on a stretch of river. Today, particularly on the chalkstreams of the
south, I would be reluctant to accept such an instruction. It would, instead,
be wise for a purchaser to form his own opinion of the value to him of
fishing a water over the next two decades. The pleasure he will experience
in entertaining his friends; in eating his own smoked salmon; in reminiscing
while seated beside his river are his to value. Why do I not wish to add
my humble opinion of the present commercial worth; of a return on capital;
of appreciation? Why mention two decades?

My reluctance is due, in part, to the commercial pressures on the river
mentioned in the Introduction. Will they reduce? Three decades will bring
us to 2020 when, in the south, we are due to experience a higher temperature
and a lower rainfall, or so the scientists predict. Consumption of energy
is rising in the world. The call for increased power releases pollution to
the skies and land and water to satisfy demand. Can organic farming pay
and thus lead the way to a reduction in the use of artificial fertilizers? Will
the decline in the salmon run be reversed in the Test? Are the spawning
areas still fit for alevins? Only a man brash with confidence, unaware of
these uncertainties, would place a capital value on a fishery and calculate
future appreciation.

Those of us who are over the top of the hill knew streams and ponds
and muddy places in the Home Counties now replaced by houses. Within
the time of my children, now in their twenties, I have seen a Dorset chalk
stream sucked almost to destruction, its soul flushed down the water pipes
of Bournemouth. Anglers and water-keepers hold well-known views on
water abstraction. Grumbles are constant on the use of artificial fertilizers
close to the river. These merit attention. It is not within the capacity of
this author to present solutions to the adverse factors bearing down on

the river. I am therefore grateful to Mick Lunn for permission to quote from his suggestion to the Test & Itchen Fishing Association in their 1988 report:

> 'Mr Lunn was certain the Test had declined and pointed to the enormous growth of flannel weed in the middle Test. He suggested a return to the old water meadows system which allowed the water from a high stream to percolate slowly through grasses and then drain away into a lower stream. He realised this is very labour intensive but thought settling lagoon/silt traps must be constructed below fish farms and cress beds and for some fisheries to have weed racks.'

If his wishes come to pass and, in addition, abstraction is reduced, our grandchildren may kneel beside the river in their turn. They will cast a fly, control the reflex lift of the rod as a black nose stretches the water skin, and feel the fusion of tension and relief as the rod settles into a lively arc. And if these restorations do not come to pass? Without doubt the river will continue to deteriorate.

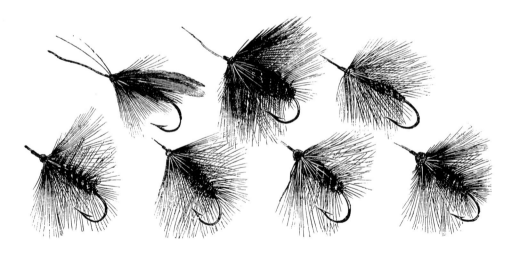

Postscript

THE RAINFALL OF DECEMBER 1989 AND JANUARY AND FEBRUARY 1990

In JANUARY AND FEBRUARY 1990 rainfall in the Test catchment area caused flooding in the middle, and particularly the lower, valley. More rain fell in those two months than in the first two months of any year, other than 1974, since 1962. My publisher asked me to assess whether this would result in any long-term improvement in the aquifer water level and river flows. On 18 January 1990 I took photographs of the dry Bourne watercourse in and below St Mary Bourne. On 26 February I re-photographed the same sites to show the rivulet in flow. Would the flow be maintained, or would abstraction dry out that little river? Would Test flows continue to reduce when surface water ran away? I sought the opinions of water-keepers in the middle and upper valley.

1 MARCH 1990 FRED KEMP – WHITCHURCH FISHERY
The recent rain brought the river over the banks in places, but in his opinion, with 17 years' experience of the Test:

> 'After four months the river will start to drop again to about 1980's summer level if there is normal rainfall. Abstraction is increasing and flow will continue to reduce.'

26 FEBRUARY 1990 ALF HARPER ——LONGPARISH HOUSE

> 'If 1990 is a normal summer for rain the extra flow will be gone by August. Two years ago we had high water – it all went in July and August. This recent rain has caused a pause in the steady decline of water volume going down the river. In recent seasons the flow rate is the same in places where the river has been reduced in width, but there is a steady reduction in volume.'

2 MARCH 1990 JEFFREY SMITH – MIDDLETON FISHERY

In late February Mrs Smith told me she had been to the Bourne valley:

> 'It was a joy to see some water in the river.'

Jeff's opinion:

> 'The river is running high but there are still mud banks. Over my 18 years on the Test I have seen a steady decline in the flow; this has been due to recent lack of rain and long-term increased abstraction. It is difficult to predict future flows because I do not know future rainfall, but if we have a reasonably normal summer I would expect the August level this year to be a little higher than in 1988. It could be right down by October. The aquifer levels are still low and more rain is needed.'

26 FEBRUARY 1990 GUY ROBINSON – LECKFORD ESTATE

When I arrived at the hatchery Guy was measuring river turbidity. In the summer of 1989 the reading was between zero and 0.002. A normal late February reading would be 0.06. On my visit the figure was 0.13 and had been as high as 0.18 after the first flush of the 1989/90 winter. The result of the increased flow and high turbidity was that he had to retain his trout fry in tanks in the hatchery beyond their normal term. Usually fry are placed out in the raceways (stews) in the first two weeks of March, but that would not be possible in 1990. Guy had experienced flooding in the recent rains, but had not lost fish from his stews 'but we had to be up and about in the night to keep the screens clear'.

Guy's prediction of summer 1990 water flows:

> 'I think this will be above the flows of 1988. Over the last 10 to 15 years there has been a slow but steady decline in flows down the valley. The present increase is likely to be temporary.'

19 FEBRUARY 1990 BRIAN PARKER – BOSSINGTON ESTATE

'I do not consider the recent high rainfall will produce anything other than a temporary improvement in water flow in the river. It is likely that we shall again have an unsatisfactory flow by this summer. I noticed that when an oak tree blew over in January that the roots were quite dry under the butt. It is no use thinking that a few weeks rain will put everything right.' Brian mentioned that Robin Crawshaw, the Fishery Officer of Southern Water had proposed a salmon parr survey. Brian suggested that instead he survey the breeding of *wild* brown trout (as opposed to stocked brown trout) of which there are few. 'If they cannot spawn in a silted river bed neither can salmon. The bed is silted for nine months of the year as the result of reduced flows, and all the little streams, where the trout used to spawn, dry out.'

I am indebted to Ron Butcher of Houghton who supplied me with the rainfall figures recorded at Bossington gardens from 1962 to 1989, and for January and February 1990.

1990
JANUARY   3.63 ins
FEBRUARY   4.37 ins
             _____
             8.00 ins

Over the 28 recorded years the first two months of 1990 were only once exceeded.

1974
JANUARY   6.71 ins
FEBRUARY   3.72 ins
             _____
             10.43 ins

Average rainfall over the 28 years period have been:

1962–65	25.95 per annum	1978–80	28.05 per annum
1966–68	29.36 per annum	1981–83	28.34 per annum
1969–71	25.56 per annum	1984–86	27.53 per annum
1972–74	28.01 per annum	1987–89	23.57 per annum
1975–77	25.88 per annum		

The average rainfall for the years 1962 to 1986 was 27.33 ins per annum.

The years 1987 to 1989 were 3.76 ins lower and would have been substantially lower without the remarkable figure of 6.65 ins in December 1989. It is clear that there was little reduction in rainfall until the three years to 1989. It would be reasonable to come to the conclusion that reduction in flows up to 1986 was due to abstraction. Thereafter reduced rainfall and abstraction were joint causes.

I quote from Ron Butcher's letter to me of 1 March 1990:

> 'The level of the river has come back to what it used to be years ago. I expect that it will drop back again. My theory is that extraction is causing a lot of the low levels during the summer. Over the past few years the winter flows have been no more than the summer flows of years ago.'